D1544677

Discard

OPRAH WINFREY

Talk Show Host and Actress

Lillie Patterson and
Cornelia H. Wright

—Contemporary Women Series—

ENSLOW PUBLISHERS, INC.

Bloy St. & Ramsey Ave.
Box 777
Hillside, N. J. 07205
U.S.A.

P.O. Box 38
Aldershot
Hants GU12 6BP
U.K.

To honor
Cornelia Patterson Green
who like Oprah's grandmother
bequeathed to her descendants
a zest for learning
and
a love of words and music.

Copyright © 1990 by Enslow Publishers, Inc.

ll rights reserved.

No part of this book may be reproduced by any means without the written permission of the publisher.

Library of Congress Cataloging-in-Publication Data

Patterson, Lillie.
    Oprah Winfrey: talk show host and actress.
    (Contemporary women series)
    Summary: Traces the life of the dynamic actress and
talk show host, from her humble beginnings in Mississippi
to her achievements in broadcasting and film.
    1. Winfrey, Oprah — Juvenile literature. 2. Television
personalities — United States — Biography — Juvenile
literature. 3. Motion picture actors and actresses —
United States — Biography — Juvenile literature.
    [1. Winfrey, Oprah. 2. Television personalities.
3. Actors and actresses. 4. Afro-Americans — Biography]
I. Wright, Cornelia H. II. Title. III. Series.
PN1992.4.W56P38   1990
791.45'092
[B]
[92]   89-17002
                                                        CIP
                                                        AC
ISBN 0-89490-289-X

Printed in the United States of America

10 9 8 7 6 5 4 3 2 1

Illustration Credits:
American Library Association, p. 109; AP/Wide World Photos, pp. 13, 22, 39, 49, 53, 70, 72, 82, 88, 96, 119; The Baltimore Sun, p. 60; The Baltimore Sun/Irving Phillips, p. 63; Ken Barboza, p. 77; Bureau of Public, Tennessee State University, p. 56; Courtesy Milwaukee Public Schools, p. 26; Nashville Banner Photo, pp. 18, 30; National Portrait Gallery, Smithsonian Institution, p. 8; Sophia Smith Collection, Smith College, p. 37; UPI/Bettmann Newsphotos, pp. 4, 102, 121.

Cover Illustration: AP/Wide World Photos.

Contents

1 Introducing Oprah 5

2 Childhood Years 6

3 A New Life in Milwaukee 15

4 Acting Out Problems 24

5 "He Saved Me" 32

6 "We've Only Just Begun!" 41

7 Lights! Camera! News! 51

8 Talking in Baltimore 58

9 At Home in Chicago 68

10 The Color Purple 75

11 The Toast of Talk 87

12 Moving with the Flow of Life . . . 100

13 Dreams and Missions 111

Chronology 125

Index 127

Oprah Winfrey

1

Introducing Oprah

Television critics describe her as a "Superstar," one of "TV's Super Women." Her dazzling smile, described as a "megawatt smile," reflects her zest for living and for meeting people.

She attracts attention with her charismatic personality. Wherever she appears, cameras click, people push to see and touch her, and reporters ask questions. Her features have become as well known as those of world leaders.

Journalists, television critics, readers, and TV viewers have described this unique woman in a multitude of ways: "friendly," "gorgeous," "refreshingly different," "mogul with a mission," "queen of talk." One gifted writer who saw her in action said she was "as dynamic as a Picasso in motion." She describes herself in simple terms: "I'm me." "Just Oprah."

Her television name, which is also her true name, is Oprah Winfrey. People from all over the United States and Canada travel to Chicago for a chance to meet her and talk, if just for a few seconds. Others meet her by watching her lively television talk show. And still other interested people learn more about this amazing black woman by reading articles and books that tell her story.

Please get to know Oprah Winfrey!

2

Childhood Years

Childhood years for Oprah were spent on a farm in Mississippi. The rural community was named for Tadeusz Kosciuszko, a name significant in American history. In later years the spelling of the Polish hero's name was simplified to Thaddeus Kosciusko.

Kosciusko came to America in 1776, during the Revolutionary War. He had studied in his native Poland and in France, and he offered his services to the colonies to help them in their fight for independence from Great Britain. He helped to design fortifications and pinpointed strategic sites for battles — work crucial to winning the war. In 1780 he was sent south to use his skills to help plan the movement of troops.

During his work in the South, Kosciusko became sympathetic to the plight of slaves who worked the huge plantations, locked in a lifetime of servitude. He believed in freedom for everyone. "I have never fought except in the cause of human freedom," he said.

Before Kosciusko left America, he made a will and left it in the care of his close friend, Thomas Jefferson. In the will, Kosciusko left his estate of land and money to Jefferson and asked him to purchase slaves with it. He wanted the slaves to be given an education and training in citizenship and "in whatever may make them happy and useful."

When Kosciusko died Thomas Jefferson had the will proved and recorded. Unfortunately, European descendants of Kosciusko contested the will, and the United States Supreme Court finally awarded the estate to them.

The Polish patriot was remembered as a beloved hero in the United States. As the nation expanded after the war, states looked for great names to give to newly settled areas in order to attract people to come and live there. A Mississippi councilman related that his grandfather served with Kosciusko. He recommended that the struggling village about seventy miles from Jackson, the state capital, be named to honor Thaddeus Kosciusko.

The community of Kosciusko developed into a place where most people were poor, but proud and hardworking. Socially, the races remained segregated, but white and black citizens lived and worked cooperatively. They helped each other with farming problems and generally did business together.

Today the town of Kosciusko is best known as the childhood home of Oprah Winfrey. She was born on January 29, 1954. The year itself is historic for two other events affecting the black race. On May 17, 1954, the U.S. Supreme Court handed down the *Brown vs. Board of Education* decision that ruled racial segregation in public schools unconstitutional.

The 1954 decision overturned the earlier *Plessy vs. Ferguson* Supreme Court ruling that had supported segregation in the United States.

Facilities for white and black Americans could be legally separate, this earlier ruling had said, so long as the facilities were equal. This "separate but equal" doctrine had kept the races separated in the Deep South in much the same manner as when slavery existed.

Thaddeus Kosciusko, Polish Army officer and statesman, and hero of the Revolutionary War

Finally, with the aid of attorneys from the National Association for the Advancement of Colored People, the problem was attacked from the focal point of education and schools. The Supreme Court's decision of 1954 recognized that "in the field of public education the doctrine of 'separate but equal' has no place. Separate educational facilities are inherently unequal."

In that same eventful year of 1954, twenty-five-year-old Dr. Martin Luther King, Jr. went to Montgomery, Alabama, as pastor of Dexter Avenue Baptist Church. By the close of the following year, the young minister had become leader of the Montgomery bus boycott that eventually inspired a South-wide freedom movement. Within a decade, most of the old customs and state laws that had robbed the black race of equal rights were being swept away by new federal legislation, or Acts of Congress. These laws eventually opened new opportunities to African Americans.

The family of the baby girl born in Kosciusko in 1954 could not know that she would grow up to play a unique role in race relations. They knew that she was special to them, and gave her a distinctive name.

That name came from the Bible, from the Book of Ruth in the Old Testament. The biblical saga tells of Naomi and her daughters-in-law, Ruth and Orpah.

Centuries later, an African-American child was named for Ruth's sister-in-law, Orpah. When the birth was recorded in the courthouse, however, the spelling of the unfamiliar name was altered. The letters "p" and "r" were reversed and the baby's name was officially recorded as Oprah, not Orpah. And that is the way the name remained—Oprah Gail Winfrey.

Baby Oprah's parents were both young. Her mother, pretty Vernita Lee, was an eighteen-year-old farm girl. Her father was tall, good-looking, twenty-year-old Vernon Winfrey. Neither of them was in a position to care for the child. Vernon Winfrey was in the armed services and stationed in Alabama. Vernita Lee did not have a paying job. She decided to follow the trend of hundreds of other blacks who were leaving the South to find jobs in the North and West. She went to Milwaukee, Wisconsin. Vernon Winfrey stayed in the Army.

It was the baby's father's mother who became "Mama" to the child. Oprah slept with Grandmother Hattie Mae in the big bed with the fluffy feather mattress familiar to many poor families in the Deep South. When Oprah Gail took her first toddling steps, she took them on the farm her grandmother owned.

Life in the rural community was quiet and happy. Grandmother Hattie Mae raised chickens and pigs. She earned enough money selling produce to buy the few necessities she did not raise or make on the farm.

There was seldom much money and no fancy frills on the farm, located at the outskirts of the town. Still, the Mississippi rural life proved a wholesome, stable environment for Oprah to spend her early childhood years in. Grandmother Hattie Mae sewed all of the little girl's clothes by hand, including the clothes Oprah wore to church on Sundays. This was not unusual for poor black families in the rural South.

Toys and other playthings were fashioned from items found on the farm, and they could be as varied and as fascinating as the child's creative genius. The fashionable china dolls with fat pink cheeks were out of the question. They cost money. In later years Oprah told how she fashioned her dolls from corncobs, the woody core of an ear of corn. These corncob dolls were popular among poor farm children.

With no other children within walking distance, little Oprah also found unusual playmates on the farm. Almost from the day she learned to walk and talk, the little girl was "on stage." She loved to talk, and she loved playacting. With her imaginative thinking, she transformed the farm animals into an audience while she talked and acted out whatever scenes came to her mind. Sometimes the characters in her playacting were imitations of the grownups who visited her grandmother.

Oprah's mother, Vernita Lee, returned to Mississippi periodically, whenever she could afford the trip. Her earnings as a cleaning woman did not permit her to come too often. Oprah's grandmother was happy to care for the lively little girl.

By the time Oprah was three, her grandmother had taught her to read. As the little girl constantly talked and used her imagination, her vocabulary expanded far beyond that of an average child her age.

Oprah's grandmother had a deep religious faith and the church was an important part of their lives. She would braid the little girl's thick, luxuriant hair and dress her in outfits she created herself. By the time Oprah was three years old, she was reciting short speeches on Christmas and Easter church programs.

Church members listened in awe when the bright-eyed, fearless little three-year-old stood up at Easter time and gave a speech on a church program. Oprah spoke about the message of Easter, telling how Jesus rose on Easter Day. From the first public speech, Oprah Gail Winfrey became a feature of special church programs.

Despite Oprah's gifts, her grandmother did not spoil her. As she grew older she had daily tasks to perform. If she failed to do them properly, she knew the consequences. Her grandmother, loving but stern, used the switch liberally. A switch was a thin branch from a bush or tree, green and supple, used for whipping children who misbehaved. Many parents in the South often made children go out and select the very switch that would be used to punish them for their mischievous behavior. The long, supple switches could zing like a whip when used by experts on bare arms or legs or buttocks. Sometimes a switching left large welts.

Oprah recalled in later years one of her grandmother's "mighty whippings" that she never forgot. Water for use indoors had to be brought from the well located several feet from their house. As soon as Oprah grew old enough to carry containers of water, her grandmother gave her the task of drawing the water from the well. One day as Oprah was carrying a bucket of water from the well to the house, she began singing a favorite popular tune to herself: "Zippidy Do-dah . . .," she sang happily, stepping to the rhythm. As she walked, she put her finger into the bucket, swirling water around and splashing as she sang. She assumed that the water would be for taking baths, not for drinking. Of course her grandmother could tell she had been playing in the water, for there stood Oprah with water dripping all over her hands. Her grandmother threatened a whipping, but nothing happened that day, or the next—or even the next. Oprah felt sure she had escaped. But punishment was often delayed.

Saturday came. Saturday was a special bath-bathing time for many poor families who lacked indoor bathrooms and took baths in large tin tubs. Oprah lugged buckets of water to heat for her Saturday-night bathing. After she had taken a relaxing bath, she stepped from the tin tub, dripping wet, and, as her grandmother would put it, "naked as a jaybird."

Suddenly her grandmother stood before her. Oprah looked at her and gave a gasp of horror when she saw the long switch in her hand. Her grandmother reminded Oprah of her misbehavior when carrying the water.

"No, Momma, no!" Oprah pleaded. She knew from experience that switches on wet skin right after a bath stung with extra pain. She kept pleading. She tried tears. None of it worked. Her grandmother saw the whippings as a way of molding Oprah's character and teaching her self-discipline. Many parents of the times used the switch in this belief. Another time Oprah got a whipping for playing in the smokehouse and knocking over a smoked ham and spilling a bag of rice all over the floor. Still another whipping was punishment for accidentally breaking a drinking glass.

Looking back over the years, Oprah has said in interviews that she knew her grandmother loved her dearly. She could trace many of her solid character traits to her formative years on the Mississippi farm. She realized later that it was her grandmother's way of showing love. "You know," she sometimes reflects, "I am what I am today because of my grandmother: my strength, my sense of

Oprah loved to playact on the rural Mississippi farm. In later years she won national acclaim as the most popular daytime show host.

reasoning, everything, all of that, was set by the time I was six years old."

Under her grandmother's rearing, strict as it was, Oprah developed into a sturdy, happy, rambunctious little girl. She created her own world there on the farm. She never owned a bicycle, but she would jump upon the back of one of the pigs and ride it bareback in rodeo fashion. She saw television programs only the few times she visited a family who owned a TV set. She had never attended a movie theater. Yet, by the time she was six years old, Oprah Winfrey showed amazing stage presence. Audiences in their rural church sat enchanted while she recited poems and stories.

Oprah enrolled in school. Her speaking and reading abilities were so advanced, she excelled in formal schooling. Her constant use of words, in reading and in playacting, seemed to make learning come easily.

At the age of six, Oprah suddenly experienced a great change in the stable rural life she had known. She traveled to an entirely different geographical location.

Her mother, Vernita Lee, decided to come and take her little girl to live with her in Wisconsin. Six-year-old Oprah Gail Winfrey began the first of several major shifts in her life.

Over the next few years, she would be taken back and forth between two distinctly different cities and become a part of households with totally different lifestyles. The story of this period is intriguing: How would this little girl adjust to these changes?

3

A New Life in Milwaukee

Summer in Milwaukee offered a dramatic change in living conditions for little Oprah Gail. Her mother, Vernita Lee, had by now spent six years in Milwaukee. She had used these years to get herself established as best she could.

Wisconsin, the eleventh largest state in the nation, stretched along the western shore of Lake Michigan. The city's population was predominantly white. Many of the families were descendants of Polish and German immigrants. Following the economic pinch of the Great Depression of the 1930s and early 1940s, many black families left the South to find employment in large cities such as Milwaukee. They often had to take low-paying menial jobs, and were thus forced to live in poverty-ridden sections of the cities.

Vernita Lee found lodging in a house owned by the godmother of a close friend. She went out each day to work as a maid, cleaning the homes of well-to-do white families who lived in affluent sections of the city. Oprah watched her mother dress carefully for work each morning. Years later she would remember the pride her mother took in the way she looked. She stepped proudly in her high-heel shoes as she went to board the bus. Her hair was always worn in a fashionable style. Her clothes were neat and as fashionable as her meager means would allow. Other bus riders would never have guessed that Vernita Lee was on her way to work as a maid.

Vernita's low wages were supplemented at times by help from the Welfare Department. By the time Oprah joined her in Milwaukee, Vernita had another baby girl. The child was cute and pretty, and all of Vernita's friends would come and make a great fuss over how adorable she was. At times, Oprah felt left out. In her impressionable young mind, she saw herself as an extra burden to her mother.

Soon Oprah was enrolled in the Milwaukee public schools. Her quick mind and ability to read well convinced her teachers that she was far too advanced to remain in the first grade where she had been placed. Oprah was skipped to the next level.

Vernita took as much pride in the way her children looked as she did in her own appearance. Even with the small public assistance, this put a heavy strain on the young mother.

Oprah's father, on the other hand, was shaping his life in a solid pattern in the South. He left the Army after he completed his service time and decided to settle down in Nashville, the state capital of Tennessee. Well-paying jobs were even more difficult for African Americans to get in the South than in the North, but Vernon Winfrey patiently worked his way upward. First he labored as a pot washer in a city hospital. Later he became a janitor at Vanderbilt University. All the while, he was preparing himself for a different kind of life in the future.

Oprah's father also fell in love with a girl named Velma. Like Vernon, she had deep religious faith. The two were married and began to put down their roots in Nashville. Vernon learned the barbering trade and later opened his own barbershop. They saved their money and began to buy real estate.

16

When his home life became secure, Vernon Winfrey asked Vernita Lee to let Oprah come and live with him in Nashville. Velma had lost the couple's first baby through miscarriage. The Winfreys longed for a child in their home.

To their delight, Vernita liked the idea. She realized that her cramped quarters in the poverty-marked surroundings of a big city would not challenge Oprah's bright mind as she grew older. Vernita Lee faced the decision of countless black mothers before her. Like them, she gave up the joy of watching a child grow up and sent the child to live in a more intellectually stimulating school environment.

So once again Oprah moved to a different geographical location. At age eight, she embarked upon another of the many chapters in her life. This one proved a happy interlude.

Velma Winfrey spent the summer helping her stepdaughter prepare to enter a new school. Oprah read far beyond her grade-school level. She had difficulty with math, however, so Velma gave her assignments every day that helped sharpen her math skills, particularly in multiplication. Velma saw to it that the scope of her reading broadened. The rule was at least one book a week, with a prescribed number of new words learned. Oprah's speaking vocabulary took on added depth. She felt completely, comfortably at home with words.

School life in Nashville challenged the alert third-grader. Her teacher recognized her gift for using words and gave her opportunities to practice it. In later years Oprah remembered how on many mornings she led the opening exercises for her class.

Vernon Winfrey found another forum for his little girl's love for giving speeches. He and Velma were devoted church workers in Nashville. Oprah resumed the churchgoing that she had known with her grandmother in Kosciusko. Once again she was performing on church programs and loving every minute of the audience applause.

During Oprah's stay in Nashville, churches were carrying on crusades to raise money to help the people of Costa Rica. This second-smallest of Central American republics was an agricultural country. Coffee, cocoa and bananas were the chief money-making crops exported to other places. Families grew most of their own food in the rich soil.

Vernon Winfrey shaped Oprah's growing years with love and firmness.

Changes came about following a series of revolutions within the country. The people of Costa Rica faced economic disaster. Many American institutions organized relief aid. Oprah worked like a little missionary, collecting pennies, nickels and dimes from her schoolmates. In her dramatic manner, she described for them the plight of the poor suffering children of Costa Rica.

Secure in her happy home life, Oprah Winfrey completed the third grade as one of the most popular children in school. She loved the limelight. In a way typical of her age group, she basked in attention from teachers and students, and the approval from Vernon and Velma Winfrey.

By the time summer came, Vernita Lee was missing her daughter. She asked Vernon Winfrey to let Oprah spend the vacation weeks in Milwaukee. Good-natured as always, he agreed. Vernon was trusting too. He did not ask for legal custody of his daughter to make sure that he would get her back.

At summer's end, he went to Milwaukee to take Oprah back to begin school. By then, however, Vernita Lee had decided to keep her daughter permanently. Vernita explained that she planned to marry the man who had been courting her for years. She could then give her children a secure home life.

Vernon Winfrey returned alone to Tennessee. In later years he recalled for a *Washington Post* reporter how he cried the day he had to leave his little girl in Milwaukee. It was the only time he ever shed tears over Oprah, he said. "I knew it was not good for her being in that environment again," he added.

He was right. The shifting from father to mother, from one section of the United States to another, caused confusion in the growing girl's life. The marriage her mother had hoped for did not take place. A baby brother had been added to the family, making living conditions even more congested. Oprah had grown old enough to feel the limitations of the stark poverty around her. Life in Milwaukee contrasted sharply with the neat homes, front porches and flower-brightened lawns of her father's Nashville neighborhood.

Oprah, being imaginative, learned to create her own world apart from the environment in which she lived. An avid reader, she could be found each day in a corner of their crowded quarters, absorbed in a book. Reading expanded her vocabulary; her world of ideas and dreams became boundless.

In addition to books, Oprah became fascinated by the television programs that were popular viewing fare in the 1960s. Television sets had become cheaper and more plentiful and even poor people could now afford them. TV series such as *Leave It To Beaver*, and *I Love Lucy* stimulated Oprah's flair for dramatic acting. The spell of television deepened for her the night she saw the gorgeous Diana Ross with her singing group, "The Supremes." There on the screen before Oprah's eyes were beautiful young girls dressed in elegant fashion, singing to national acclaim. And they were *black*! They were stars! Oprah's creative mind began to spin fanciful dreams for her own future.

The dreams could well have been shattered by traumatic experiences. When her mother had to be away, she often left Oprah in the care of babysitters. Over the years some of these male babysitters molested her.

In later years, Oprah described her fright and confusion. She did not know what to do. Like so many young girls who are forced into this terrifying experience, she felt that grownups would blame her. Children are often too confused to know how to go and explain such an incident to an adult. Afraid that her mother might blame and punish her, Oprah kept silent.

During a session of her *A.M. Chicago* show, however, Oprah talked about this episode in her life. That day's program dealt with the topic of women who had at some time suffered abuse. When one guest became overwrought in trying to tell her story, Oprah let her know that she, too, had faced molestation.

In an interview later for *Essence* magazine, Oprah said: "Although I probably wouldn't have chosen that way to share it, it has certainly done a lot of good for a lot of people." After Oprah's acknowledgment on the *A.M. Chicago* program, the studio received nearly a thousand letters from viewers who wrote to say how much Oprah's remarks had helped them.

Her own life experiences later inspired Oprah to give time and money to help youngsters who are confused or misdirected. She encourages them to look to the present and the future, rather than dwell upon negative things that happened in the past. The emphasis, she advises, should be upon *overcoming* problems of the past and growing toward the future.

The television industry continued to make revolutionary changes during Oprah's growing years. Modernization of television equipment led to wide popularity of TV sets. Picture screens were made larger. The sets became more affordable. At the flick of a switch, events could be viewed in homes. The addition of color to the televised pictures made programs more understandable, and more enjoyable.

By the 1960s more TV programs were being sent over longer distances than ever before. Americans could watch history as it was being made. The dramatic progress of the Freedom Movement, inspired by Dr. Martin Luther King, Jr., was watched daily like episodes in a continuing serial. TV viewers saw Dr. King mature from a young Montgomery minister to become a national leader. They saw teenage students stun the world as they staged "sit-ins" at lunch counters that refused to serve black citizens, and remained peaceful even when they were spat upon by whites. TV cameras later relayed pictures of the Freedom Ride that ended segregation in interstate travel, and of the campaigns that won protection of the right to vote for all citizens. Oprah Winfrey grew up during a time of drastic changes and fast-paced events.

The years were times of tragedy as well as triumph. Viewers saw churches burned, and people being killed. Young, handsome President John Fitzgerald Kennedy was shot while he rode in a motorcade through the streets of Dallas, Texas. His younger

The original Supremes captivated Oprah's attention and influenced her love affair with television.

brother, Robert Francis Kennedy, who later became a popular presidential candidate, was shot in a hotel after giving a stirring speech.

The turbulent 1960s was an era of opportunities for African-American students. The integration of schools in southern states put an end to the customs and local laws that prevented athletic competition and social interaction between white and black students. Dark-complexioned competitors were soon a naturally accepted part of television entertainment. Scholarships to previously all-white schools became available, for academic as well as for athletic excellence.

These years brought excitement to African-American students with big goals for their lives and a willingness to work toward these goals. For students with keen intellectual abilities and great dreams, future success could be limitless.

Oprah said in later years, "I used to say that when I grew up I wanted to be Diana Ross, Tina Turner, and Maya Angelou rolled into one."

Young Oprah Winfrey had the intelligence, but she began to think that her dreams would have to be deferred.

What happens to a dream deferred? Many things can happen, according to the African-American poet Langston Hughes. A dream can "dry up like a raisin in the sun," or, "it can explode." It would have been hard to say, at this point in Oprah's life, which of these two outcomes was the more likely.

Fortunately for Oprah Gail Winfrey, her life would take several amazing turns.

4

Acting Out Problems

Oprah entered her teen years still in Milwaukee with her mother. She was growing up fast, mentally and physically. At age thirteen, her body had begun to develop into shapely curves. Her thinking and speaking abilities were advanced for her age and school level.

She entered high school earlier than usual because of the grades she had skipped. Lincoln High, the secondary school nearest her home, had many of the problems typical of upper-level public schools in large cities where poor families live. Schools seemed unable to motivate the students. Behavior was often rowdy. Oprah tried to retreat into a world of reading.

Discerning teachers recognized that Oprah's creative mind was not being challenged. One of the teachers helped her to get a full scholarship to Nicolet High School. This was an exclusive private school located in one of Milwaukee's suburban areas. Oprah became one of the few non-white students enrolled.

More and more expensive private schools were offering scholarships to minority students. After the Supreme Court ruled in 1954 that segregated schools were illegal, thoughtful school officials tried to make up for years of neglecting the education of minority students. Selected students who showed potential for achievement, but whose families had little money, were sought by schools that had never considered black students. These students were granted scholarships, with all expenses paid.

Wealthy white students at Nicolet vied for the black girl's friendship. Their affectionate name for her was "Opie." Schoolmates took her to their posh homes to meet their families. At that time, it was definitely chic to have black friends if you were white and rich. White mothers invited Oprah for lunch and tea.

So the early 1960s proved to be a wonderful time for talented young black people like Oprah Winfrey.

For Oprah—to quote *A Tale of Two Cities* by Charles Dickens—"It was the best of times, it was the worst of times." It was the best of times because most of her schoolmates had high intellectual goals, and a background of travel and good schooling. Oprah was challenged, and she made top-notch grades. Socially, she developed genuine friendships.

Yet these outwardly pleasant experiences also caused problems for a sensitive teenager. Oprah had to catch buses to get from Nicolet to her home. The long ride gave her daily reminders of the differences between her lifestyle and those of her schoolmates. The neighborhoods of the rich had spacious homes, lush lawns, trees and flowering plants. By the time Oprah reached her own neighborhood, she said later, "It was like going back to Cinderella's house from the castle every night."

Oprah was forced to face the hard truth that in a world of haves and have-nots, she belonged to the latter group. She was *poor*! For the bright, ambitious teenager, the realization brought on frustrations. There was no way her mother could give her the things that would allow her to keep pace with her school friends. It was tough going for Vernita just to make ends meet.

Oprah felt painted into a corner. She began to rebel, to lash out. Like any teenager, she wanted some of the things her schoolmates had, and when they invited her to go with them for pizza and shakes after school, she wanted to have money to go — and to treat them sometimes. Frustrated by the barriers that poverty seemed to place in her path, Oprah began to act out her frustrations in first one way, then another. Vernita Lee could not understand what was happening to her daughter.

Aerial view of Lincoln High School, Milwaukee, Wisconsin, where Oprah began her high school studies.

The problems were only beginning. Gradually, as crisis after crisis arose, Vernita began to wonder whether she could cope with the rebellious moods.

Thinking back to this period later, Oprah recalled, "I started acting out my need for attention, my need to be loved." And she could act!

One critical incident came about because of her need to wear eyeglasses. When doctors examined Oprah's eyes, they discovered that she had imperfect vision. Her eyes were not focusing properly. The doctor recommended prescription eyeglasses, with bifocal lenses. These lenses would be ground to two different focal lengths, with one part for close focus, for reading.

Oprah's mother saved up the money and bought the prescription glasses. But when Oprah looked at herself in the mirror, she thought she looked ugly. The glasses had frames shaped like butterflies at the corners. Some people thought this style was fashionable, but Oprah hated it. She wanted to have stylish expensive glasses like the ones her friends at school wore. She pleaded with her mother to buy another pair. Of course Vernita could not do so. She had barely saved enough to buy the first pair.

The more she thought about the eyeglasses, Oprah recalled, the more she hated them. Somehow, she had to get rid of them. At this point, Oprah's dramatic instincts took over. Many years later she would recall how she decided upon a daring plan. She staged a drama to get rid of the hated bifocals. She had already worked the whole scene out in her mind. First she threw the bifocal "butterfly" glasses to the floor. Second she stomped on the lenses until she had smashed them into tiny pieces. She yanked down the curtains, knocked over lamps, and ransacked the apartment until it was in complete disarray.

Then, as she later told it, she telephoned the police, lay down on the floor and waited for them to come.

By the time the officers arrived, Oprah was ready to give a stunning performance of an amnesia victim. She had watched popular television series that told about someone who suffered from amnesia, a gap in memory. If she pretended to have amnesia, she could pretend to have no recollection of what had happened.

The story sounded implausible, but the police rushed her to the hospital. The hospital doctors wanted to reach her mother. Oprah pretended she could not remember anything. The faked amnesia kept her silent. "Who are you?" the doctors asked over and over. Oprah pretended to be faint. The acting was superb.

Eventually the police located Vernita Lee at work; she arrived at the hospital nearly hysterical, thinking her daughter had been seriously hurt. The lawmen described the scene in the apartment when they arrived. They mentioned the smashed eyeglasses. By this time Oprah had become scared. She was still pretending she did not even know her mother.

Vernita quickly saw through the scenario. Anger replaced her tears. She spoke in a quiet, measured voice. Oprah recognized the tone of voice; it spelled trouble. "I'm going to count to three," Vernita said, "and see if your memory improves." She began counting. By the time she counted to two, Oprah blinked her eyes as though fighting to recall something. Before Vernita counted to three, Oprah knew the act was over. "You're my *mother!*" she cried out. "You're my *mother!*"

At school Oprah kept up her high level of scholastic achievement, and she made friends easily. At home, however, she continued to dramatize the need for challenges her environment did not offer.

The most outrageous drama took Oprah away from her mother. She decided to run away from it all. Looking back later, Oprah would recall these antics with characteristic humor, and display her ability to laugh at herself.

The idea seemed neat when Oprah first thought about it. She stuffed some belongings in a shopping bag and headed for the home of her best girlfriend. She planned to stay with the friend and her family for a time. Maybe the two of them could later run away together. The plan fell flat. When Oprah rapped on the door, nobody answered. She did not know that her girlfriend had taken a trip with her family.

Now what? Oprah was afraid to return home. Lugging her shopping bag, she walked the streets and tried to figure out her next move. Eventually she found herself in the downtown section. As she stood watching the sights, her eyes focused upon a sleek limousine as it pulled up before a hotel. As she looked on in fascination, a stylishly dressed woman stepped out. Oprah recognized the woman as Aretha Franklin, the famous black singer from Detroit. Aretha's father pastored a large Detroit church, and she had once sung in his church choir. From there she became a stage and recording artist. Oprah immediately became the actress. By the time she reached Aretha Franklin, she was crying pitifully. The story she told was heartbreaking. Oprah spun a yarn about being left by her parents in Milwaukee. She was stranded, she sobbed, with no money to return home to Ohio. She had no place to go. The sad story must have touched Aretha Franklin. Oprah was so convincing that the singer-star asked no questions, but gave Oprah one hundred dollars.

One hundred dollars! Oprah's spirits revived. The money inspired her to continue her adventure. She went to a nearby hotel and rented a room. It seemed so glamorous! She ordered room service and had a grand time. By the next day, however, the adventure of running away did not seem such a wonderful idea. She felt lonely for home, yet she was afraid to return and face her mother. She stayed on in the hotel, and the money dwindled. Soon it was all gone, and Oprah had to leave the hotel.

Oprah's talents blossomed as a high school student in Nashville, Tennessee.

At this point, Oprah was helped by the religious training her grandmother had given her. She asked her minister to help. He went home with Oprah and helped her face her mother. He could not change Vernita's mind on one point, however: she had decided that she could no longer cope with her brilliant, high-spirited adolescent daughter. Vernita decided that the place for Oprah was a juvenile detention home. She took Oprah there, down to Juvenile Services. Fortunately for Oprah, and for history, there was no space. There were too many other young people who needed help. Vernita was told to bring her daughter back in two weeks.

The delay decided Oprah Winfrey's fate. Vernita Lee returned home and dialed a telephone number. The voice that answered the call was that of Vernon Winfrey. Oprah's mother explained the situation.

The young girl's fate hung on the way her father responded. As it turned out, her father was a no-nonsense man of action. Without hesitation, he had a solution. His daughter must not go to a juvenile home, Vernon Winfrey told Vernita. Oprah's home would be with him—with her father in Nashville, Tennessee.

Once again, Oprah Winfrey had a change in living environment during her developing years. This time she came under the guidance of someone who understood her behavior. Moreover, he knew how to deal with it. In many ways, Oprah and her father were alike. She spoke of this years later in an interview for *Parade* magazine: "It took me a while to figure it out, but there are no two ways about it," she said, "I am definitely my father's child."

In 1968, the creative, rambunctious teenager finally met her match.

5

"He Saved Me"

"When my father took me, he changed the course of my life. He saved me."

This high praise from Oprah Winfrey gives credit to Vernon Winfrey for helping to guide her through her teen years. Her father recognized her problems. This pretty, willful girl simply needed discipline and channels for her talents and boundless creative energies. Most of all she needed love and a sense of security.

Vernon Winfrey did not waste time. His easygoing manner and friendly smile did not belie a firmness and iron will. He understood his daughter, and he knew exactly how to point her nose in a positive direction.

First off, he insisted that some of the "hip" talk and dress and actions she had acquired had to go. He set her straight about the way she addressed him.

When Oprah returned to Nashville, she began calling her father "Pops." Vernon Winfrey later explained his reaction. "Oprah, honey," he told her, "you were Gail or Oprah when you left, right? And I was Daddy when you left and I'm gonna be Daddy since you're back I will not accept the word 'Pops.'" From then on, Oprah called him Daddy.

Father and daughter reached an understanding about a proper dress code. Like any youngster, Oprah instinctively knew that many pranks she could get away with in one setting simply wouldn't be tolerated in another. Her father never once threatened to whip her. He had a way of tilting his chin down low and then slowly giving her a sidelong glance. That signal was enough for Oprah.

Beneath the strict rules, though, she could sense the caring.

Vernon Winfrey's "ammunition" consisted of reasonable discipline, consistency, structure, unwavering standards, and love. By the time Oprah had been with him six months, there were changes in her attitude as well as in her dress.

Vernon Winfrey studied his daughter's style of wearing clothes and knew it was time for a talk. The short tight-fitting skirts had to go. With them went the halter tops that bared her shoulders and upper back. He took his daughter shopping and bought clothes suitable for a high-school student to wear.

He even checked her makeup. Oprah had formed the habit of wearing heavy makeup that her father believed inappropriate for her age. Vernon Winfrey did not fuss and fume. Instead, he gently helped her wipe most of the makeup away. Her naturally clear brown skin looked more beautiful without the artificial layers of cosmetics.

Oprah's father not only demanded obedience, he also wanted it promptly, and without any lip from his daughter. She learned one of his favorite sayings, and years later both of them could repeat it. "Listen girl," he would say, "If I tell you a mosquito can pull a wagon, don't ask me questions, just hitch him up."

The concerned parenting helped Oprah with her studies. She had a brilliant mind and showed leadership possibilities. She needed to learn how to direct her natural talents toward her overall development.

HEBRON PUBLIC SCHOOL LIBRARY

Vernon Winfrey insisted that his daughter's grades in school reflect her abilities. The day she brought a report card home with a grade of "C" her father let her know that for her, this low mark was not acceptable.

Oprah tried to make her point. After all, a C was considered a passing grade. Yes, for some students, her father answered. For his daughter, no. She could do better. Therefore, a grade of C was not acceptable from her.

After that talk, Oprah began bringing home A's. She learned to take pride in her intelligence, and the fact that her name was listed on the honor role regularly.

Within a short time, Oprah learned that it was useless to try and see how much she could get away with. She did a complete turnabout and began to show how much she could accomplish in a short time.

Velma and Vernon Winfrey could afford to give their daughter a comfortable home, along with the guidance and caring. He had worked hard, and the barbershop he had started four years earlier was doing well. He had bought a house in a clean, cheerful neighborhood. Oprah now had the security of knowing that she would no longer have to move back and forth from Milwaukee to Nashville.

Love and trust and a firm base were really there for her support. Oprah learned to respect Vernon Winfrey's guidance. Oprah said of her father, "He knew what he wanted and expected, and he would take nothing less."

School life for black students had changed in the South. By 1968, most southern states were attempting to comply with the 1954 United States Supreme Court decision to end forced segregation in schools. Most cities began school integration at the high-school level. Despite delays, and protests from segregationists, young people were adapting to the new policy.

In Nashville, Tennessee, East High School had begun to admit black students. Oprah became one of the few black students enrolled there. Since she had been attending integrated schools in Milwaukee, she adapted easily to the interracial setting. In fact she was happier, because East High did not have the wide gap between many rich whites and a few poor blacks that existed at Nicolet in Milwaukee.

Oprah developed self-confidence in her own unique qualities.

It took only a short period for the vivacious, outgoing girl to become a student leader at East High. With her newfound self-assurance, she took an active role in school life. The dramatic talent she had used in Milwaukee to stage stunts were used at East High to enrich school programs. The joy of speaking before audiences that had begun during childhood days in Kosciusko, Mississippi, now returned. Oprah played acting roles in school dramas. She would have the high-school students and teachers mesmerized by the spirit and passion of her performances.

Oprah especially enjoyed interpreting selections that showed the power and strength of black women, whether as writers, book characters, or heroines of history. The reading of library books, always encouraged by Velma Winfrey, helped Oprah to learn more about the courageous black women of American history. Oprah developed a fascination for these women, and for the writers who recreated their life stories.

A favorite author for Oprah during high school was Maya Angelou. Her real name was Margaret, but her brother nicknamed her Maya meaning "mine."

Maya Angelou wrote the story of her own life in the bestseller, *I Know Why the Caged Bird Sings.* Like Oprah, Maya was cared for by her grandmother in a small southern community. Her autobiography tells of her growing years, her successful battle with painful experiences, and her triumph as a world-famous dancer, author and speaker. During the 1960s Maya Angelou worked in the

North to gain support for Dr. Martin Luther King's Civil Rights Crusade for Justice and Freedom in America.

Religious training, like reading, added richness to Oprah's maturing years. Both Vernon and Velma Winfrey were ardent church workers. Oprah joined them, taking up the zeal she had known when she attended church in Kosciusko. The church folk loved her. They could always count on her to perform on church programs.

The year Oprah celebrated her sixteenth birthday, she was voted the most popular girl in her class. Students liked her for her school spirit as well as her talents. She liked people. And she liked to talk.

Oprah's father continued to guide his daughter with a firm hand, and he praised her for the way she had taken control of her life. It was wonderful to be voted the most popular, he told her. He also added a bit of advice for her to remember. It would be even greater to be considered the student most likely to succeed. Oprah remembered those words of wisdom.

The church, as well as the school, gave Oprah a forum to speak and to perform dramatic readings. Oprah held church audiences spellbound when she assumed the role of Sojourner Truth, an ex-slave who became one of those early Americans who dared to speak out for the rights of women. Her provocative life story makes exciting reading for young and old alike.

Sojourner Truth was born a slave in Ulster County, New York in 1797, and given the name Isabella. She was sold from one slave owner to another, and finally became free when New York State abolished slavery.

One day, Isabella said, she asked God for a new name to use in freedom, and God gave her two names. One name was Sojourner, symbolizing that she would sojourn, travel about the country to speak out to people. Her second name was Truth, symbolizing what she would tell people: Truth. Sojourner Truth was described as calm

Sojourner Truth, outspoken feminist and freedom fighter.

and erect, like "one of the native palm trees waving alone in the desert."

Sojourner spoke out against the enslavement of her race. And she became the first black woman to speak publicly for the rights of all women. At a time when women were crusading for the right to vote, she became a powerful speaker for the cause, even though she had never been taught to read or write.

One of Sojourner's best known appearances came during the second convention of the women's suffrage movement, held in Akron, Ohio, in 1852. In one session men were ridiculing the idea of equal rights, saying women were weak, and had to be helped into carriages, and could not do manual labor.

Suddenly Sojourner stepped to the platform and spoke the truth. She stood, tall and regal, and looked at the assembly.

"Don't let her speak!" scores of delegates rose and shouted — "*Don't let her speak!*"

Sojourner listened to God, not to white folks; she spoke. Her deep voice filled the hall with a speech that became a classic of the suffrage movement.

"Nobody ever helped *me* into carriages, or *over* mud puddles" — she reared back and thundered the words — "and ain't I a woman?"

Sojourner repeated the rhythmic question as she spoke, while the audience cheered, "Yes! Yes!"

"I have born'd five children and seen them most all sold off into slavery, and when I cried out with mother's grief, none but Jesus heard — *and ain't I a woman?*"

At the close of her speech, the white feminists jumped to their feet, waving their handkerchiefs and cheering the ex-slave. Sojourner stood for a moment, quietly watching them. Finally she smiled and said quietly, "Obliged to ye for hearing me."

Oprah literally "became" Sojourner Truth when she gave the

Maya Angelou, author, poet, playwright, editor, Oprah's trusted mentor and confidante.

"Ain't I a Woman" speech. Crowds cheered her as they had cheered Sojourner.

The words and life stories of strong women such as Sojourner Truth and Maya Angelou helped Oprah Winfrey to begin refining her own public-speaking style. Learning about these women also helped the teenager develop a sense of direction for her life.

In later years Oprah would acknowledge how the story of these strong black women helped her to grow and develop. She called their legacy "the bridges that I've crossed over to get where I am."

By the year 1970, Oprah, now sixteen, had developed into quite a leader at East High. Her school friends persuaded her to enter the race for the presidency of the student council, one of the most prestigious elected positions in a high school.

Oprah accepted the challenge. This took nerve for a black girl in the South with predominantly white schoolmates. Oprah worked to keep the racial issue out of the campaign. Instead, she analyzed the major gripes of the students and built her campaign around these concerns. She promised to work for better cafeteria food. Another of her campaign pledges was the improvement of school spirit among the student body.

Oprah, ever innovative, even dared to promise a live band for the junior-senior prom. Past proms were held in the school gymnasium, and students danced to recorded music. This was the custom. The idea of a live band thrilled the seniors.

Oprah Winfrey won the election. The girl, who, but for a quirk of fate, would have ended up in a detention home, became president of the student council at the predominantly white East High School. One exciting experience after another seemed to be propelling her toward a unique destiny.

6

"We've Only Just Begun!"

The 1970s began as a seemingly magical time for Oprah Winfrey. She continued to excel as a student at East High. The school chose her as one of the Outstanding Teenagers of America.

More exciting adventures followed. She was invited to join teenagers from all over the United States to attend the 1970 White House Conference on Youth. The White House conferences were convened by presidents of the United States to discuss a wide range of problems. The 1970 conference met in Estes Park, California, to discuss problems concerning young people. Oprah was selected because of her high grades in school and her leadership in school and community life. She joined other selected teenagers, as well as adult leaders, as they discussed solutions to problems affecting the lives of young people.

Vernon Winfrey encouraged his daughter, and guided her with his usual steady philosophy. In later years his voice still reflected pride when he talked to interviewers about this period in his daughter's life. "When she was sixteen," he recalls, "she went to Los Angeles to speak at a church."

The trip became an adventure for Oprah. While in California, she had the chance to visit Hollywood, the district of Los Angeles considered the motion-picture capital of the world. She walked along famous Hollywood Boulevard, and stopped to admire the famous old Grauman's Chinese Theater, built in the shape of a Chinese pagoda. According to a longstanding ritual, famous movie stars leave their footprints, handprints, and signatures engraved in the cement in front of Grauman's Theater.

The high-school girl from Nashville gazed in awe upon the names of the movie stars. The visit became a very special moment in her life.

When Oprah returned to Nashville, she told her parents about all the exciting things she had seen and done. Vernon Winfrey later shared his daughter's unusual experience in an interview for *The Nashville Banner*, the city's newspaper. "Daddy," Oprah said, "I got down on my knees there and ran my hand along all those stars on the street and I said to myself, 'One day, I'm going to put my own star among those stars.' "

Her father had a foreshadowing feeling then, he said, that "she would one day be famous."

Oprah still found time for church work and community projects. She participated in the yearly local walkathons to raise money in the March of Dimes Campaign. Like other participants, she persuaded sponsors to pledge a certain amount of money for every mile she covered in the walkathon. The money raised helped in the prevention of birth defects. Ever competitive, Oprah looked for as many sponsors as possible. One day she went to radio station WVOL, not far from her home. The producer, John Heidelberg, promised to become a sponsor in the walkathon.

This was the beginning of a totally surprising turn of events. After the walkathon, Oprah returned to the WVOL station to collect the money John Heidelberg had pledged. He too was from Mississippi. As the two talked together, John Heidelberg listened to the expressive quality in Oprah's voice. He was so impressed, he asked her if she had ever considered a career in radio broadcasting. Oprah had not. John Heidelberg then asked if she would like to hear her voice on tape. "Sure," Oprah answered.

John Heidelberg then took Oprah into a newsroom and handed her some copy off the news wire.

Oprah stepped to a mike and began reading. John Heidelberg listened. Soon other studio personnel stopped by and listened. When Oprah finished and the tape was played back, she listened with them. Later, the engineer complimented Oprah on her reading, and added, "And the mike loves your voice."

The demonstration tape was played for the station manager, then for staff members. They all liked it. Still a lingering doubt caused some of them to question hiring a girl still in high school. In the end they decided to try Oprah on a part-time basis. In the early 1970s women, particularly African-American women, were only just beginning to find success in news broadcasting.

Oprah faced one more hurdle before she could be hired. She had to hear from Vernon Winfrey. As expected, Oprah's father had questions. He debated whether a radio station was a proper environment for a high-school girl. He wanted his gifted daughter to have a successful career.

John Heidelberg persuaded Vernon Winfrey that Oprah would be safe with them. Also, he reminded him, this opportunity might just be the beginning of a great career. He finally won Vernon Winfrey's permission and promised to take care of Oprah.

At age seventeen, the high-school senior began working part-time at radio station WVOL. The station was not far from her home. At first, she worked as a trainee and received no pay. Oprah loved the experience, and she made the most of it.

A new day was dawning for women and for African Americans in the media. The crusade for equality and justice led by Dr. Martin Luther King, Jr. had resulted in what became known as affirmative action programs, designed to promote the acceptance of minorities by medical schools, special training programs, industries, etc., that had previously ignored them. All business and institutional employers were expected to comply with affirmative action. The civil rights movement of the 1960s brought greater equality not only to African Americans, but also to women, handicapped persons, and other groups who had not previously received fair consideration, especially in job opportunities.

At station WVOL, Oprah Winfrey was trained to read the late afternoon and early evening news. It was a whirlwind existence. She still participated in school activities. Afternoons, she rushed from school to her radio station to prepare for her broadcast assignment. She read the news at 3:30, and at half-hour intervals until 8:00 in the evening. It was a hectic, heady existence. Oprah's enthusiasm showed that she loved every minute of it.

Her social and intellectual world expanded. As a radio personality, she became more involved in community and charitable functions. This included fundraising activities to help destitute families. In addition, she continued to perform readings on church programs.

One unusual experience for Oprah seemed to flow naturally into another. The station manager of WVOL, impressed by the work of firemen who tried to save his burning house, decided to participate in the annual Miss Fire Prevention contest, sponsored by the local fire department.

The choosing of Miss Fire Prevention always created excitement every year in Nashville. Many businesses and organizations selected a beautiful teenage girl to sponsor. In past years, contestants had usually been beauties with red or blond hair, and they had always been white.

Station WVOL decided to sponsor Oprah Winfrey. Oprah did not have blond or red hair. What she had was plenty of nerve, and her own unique brand of loveliness. She also had poise, and confidence in her winning chances. At age seventeen, she had developed into quite a beauty, with large, wide-spaced eyes that seemed to dance, especially when she smiled. And when she flashed that broad smile, people could see the resemblance to Vernon Winfrey.

At one point in the Miss Fire Prevention contest, each of the contestants was interviewed by the panel of judges. The way each girl answered affected her overall score.

Oprah's turn came. The judges asked her what she wanted to do with her life. Oprah's reply showed how much she had matured. "I believe in truth," she told the judges, "and I want to perpetuate truth. So I want to be a journalist."

The answer impressed the judges. Oprah moved on to the next level of the contest. She stayed in the running until the very last round before the judges picked the finalist. Only three girls were left. Oprah was one of them.

Each of the three girls had to answer questions posed by the judges. Their answers would determine their final score.

"What would you do," the judges asked each girl, "if you suddenly came into possession of one million dollars?"

One finalist considered her family. She would buy her mother a refrigerator, her father a truck, and her brother a motorcycle, she told the judge.

The second contestant had a noble reply. She would give the entire fortune away to help the poor.

That left Oprah. How could she possibly think up an answer more impressive than the ones already given? She chose to be brash and creative. "If I had a million dollars," she began in her deep, expressive voice, then paused before she exclaimed, "I'd be a spending *fool*." Oprah spoke honestly — and in such an amusing fashion that she won the contest.

Nashville had its first black Miss Fire Prevention. And the winner was steadily paving the way to her future career.

Meanwhile, Oprah helped plan graduation activities at East

High. The senior prom was one of the grand moments for graduating seniors. At East High, as in many southern high schools, the prom was still held in the gymnasium, but Oprah saw to it that decorations transformed the gym into a gala dance hall.

She was a key member of the decorating team for her class. The invitation to the prom publicized their theme: "An Evening Above the Clouds." For that evening of May 7, 1971, Oprah and her decorating committee had blue, silver, and white paper giving the illusion of a heavenly scene, with shining stars suspended from paper clouds.

The prom escort for the most popular girl was the most popular boy at East High. He was Anthony Otey, a good-looking honor student with a broad, disarming grin.

Oprah and Anthony had struck up a firm friendship. Vernon Winfrey knew that his adored daughter had grown up. He allowed her to go with Otey on dates. The two went to movies and concerts. Sometimes, as they took long walks through the lovely city parks, they shared the ambitions each had for the future. Anthony had already won prizes for art and dreamed of becoming an artist. Oprah set her sights on becoming a great actress.

The prom evening "Above the Clouds" was an exquisite one for Oprah and her classmates. She had kept to her promises; the students danced to the music of a *live* band. Even Vernon Winfrey sensed the importance of the event in the life of a student. He gave Oprah permission to stay out after twelve o'clock.

The motto for the 1971 graduating class of East High was true enough of Oprah Winfrey's future: "We've only just begun!" Oprah Winfrey's life seemed to advance in clear-cut stages; she was about to enter a new one.

The choice of a college is a major decision in any person's life. Which college would be best for Oprah? The question occasioned long discussions in the Winfrey household. On the one hand, Oprah wanted to get away from Nashville. On the other, she enjoyed radio broadcasting. Oprah and her father debated the pros and cons of leaving or staying in Nashville, a city that boasted a number of excellent colleges and universities.

Father and daughter reached a sensible plan. Oprah agreed to go to college in Nashville. The matter of which college was settled when she received a scholarship to Tennessee State University, given by the local Elks Club. Tennessee State University (TSU) was noted for solid studies in speech and drama. It was also less than seven miles from the Winfrey home. This made it possible for Oprah to continue her part-time broadcasting at station WVOL.

Oprah Winfrey entered college still not sure of a major. Her father had his mind set on her becoming a teacher, traditionally one of the most highly respected professions among blacks in the South. Oprah still nurtured her dream of becoming an actress.

At TSU, professors began to guide her career. Dr. Thomas E. Poag, the first black scholar to receive a master's and Ph.D. degree in theater arts in the United States, had established the speech-theater department at the college. Dr. Poag knew dramatic talent when he saw it. He saw it in Oprah Winfrey, and encouraged her to major in speech and drama.

Oprah's schedule would seem hectic to most college freshmen. She went to her college classes during the early hours of the day. In the afternoon she went to broadcast at station WVOL. Fortunately, she had learned to drive and had a car. The radio station was located between home and school, which made it convenient for Oprah to travel to all three places.

Another professor who influenced Oprah's college training was Dr. Jamie Williams, who taught oral interpretation. Dr. Williams stressed the importance of enthusiasm when communicating with any audience.

Oprah learned this lesson well. "She was a joy!" Dr. Williams told interviewers in later years. "Students thoroughly enjoyed coming to class and listening to her."

Work and studies were not all that kept the college freshman busy. Oprah continued to participate in beauty pageants.

In the spring of 1972, Oprah Winfrey entered the Miss Black Nashville contest. She won. This was the first step toward the Miss Black America pageant. The next round would pick Miss Black Tennessee. Oprah knew that she would be up against other beauties, so she concentrated upon her other assets, such as poise and talent. She won again and this time she was crowned Miss Black Tennessee.

Next — on to California, to vie for the Miss Black America title. As a state winner, all of Oprah's expenses were paid. With her zest for life, she was determined to enjoy every moment of the trip.

The format for Miss Black America was similar to that of the Miss America pageant, which at that time did not consider black girls for inclusion. Dark-skinned Americans, however, were redefining their concept of the qualities to consider in choosing a beauty queen. Physical beauty was no longer looked upon as synonymous with fair skin and silky hair. Each racial group has unique physical features that constitute unique beauty. The judges for Miss Black America considered the overall girl, including her talents and personality.

Each girl was accompanied by a chaperone who advised her and looked out for her welfare during the contest. Dr. Janet Burch, a highly-regarded Nashville psychologist, was asked to accompany Oprah as her chaperone.

In California, Oprah made friends with the other state contestants during the social events. She reveled in the excitement of shopping for new clothes. The contestants were invited to parties, and met Hollywood celebrities. This time, Oprah had the chance to chat with the stars in person.

Miss Black Tennessee, Oprah Winfrey, did not win the national contest. But she won other things that were, for her, perhaps more important. She knew that her dramatic routine in the talent portion held the audience in awed silence. During that California trip, Oprah made a promise to her chaperone, and to herself. One day, she predicted, she was going to be a star as famous as the ones they met in Hollywood.

College studies, broadcasting at WVOL, beauty contests,

Oprah Winfrey and James Earl Jones, famed actor, both national activists in community service.

public appearances—all these kept Oprah on the go. As a result, she did not take part in the usual college campus activities. She did not become a student leader as she had been in high school.

During the early 1970s, many college students still continued the protests for social changes that students had demonstrated and died for during the sixties. Oprah did not join in the protest demonstrations. She explained her position then, and in later years. Her entire life, Oprah says, celebrates her blackness, and her striving to excel is what best honors her people.

7

Lights! Camera! News!

In the fall of 1973, station WTVF-TV, Nashville's Channel 5, was searching for an anchorperson. WTVF was the local outlet for the Columbia Broadcasting System (CBS), one of the three major television networks. (A network operates by linking together many stations.) The station knew of Oprah Winfrey's work in radio. Chris Clark, WTVF's news director, asked if she would come and audition for the job.

The invitation caught Oprah by surprise. For a student still in college, the offer was mind-boggling. Television? She decided she needed advice. Besides, she had her heart set on becoming an actress, not working in television.

First, she had a long talk with John Heidelberg. She was still working part-time with him at WVOL. He had taken a chance with her as a novice and she did not want to appear ungrateful.

John Heidelberg urged her to go on and try for the position. Television stations were hiring black people in more responsible and visible roles in their programming.

Would she be letting him down to leave the radio station, Oprah worried. John Heidelberg counseled her to go for the audition – to "go as far as your talent will take you."

Oprah telephoned the television station and made an appointment. She began to plan what she would do or say during an audition for television. Years later she shared with a television audience her feelings the day she went for her first audition for a television job. She was a nervous wreck, Oprah confessed. To steady her nerves she decided to pretend that she was one of her favorite television personalities. In a male-dominated profession, Barbara Walters had become the only woman to rise to the position of co-anchor on a national network news program. She was especially admired for her talent in conducting interviews.

When Oprah made her audition tape, she said she pretended to be Barbara Walters. She had watched Walters on television over and over. So she sat like Barbara, and crossed her ankles, and leaned across the desk, just the way Barbara did. Actually, Oprah had the poise and talent herself to hold her own. In the audition, Chris Clark reported later, she came across as – Oprah Winfrey.

The WTVF news director studied the tape and summed up his opinion in one word: "Wow!" Oprah looked great on camera. Her deep rich voice had an easy-to-listen-to quality that would please television audiences. She spoke with an air of authority, yet she also communicated warmth and friendliness.

Oprah left the television station not knowing what the outcome of her audition would be. Later, Chris Clark telephoned her and offered her the position.

Before she gave an answer, Oprah went to talk to Dr. William Cox, a professor whose opinion she respected. She told Dr. Cox about the television offer. "I need you to help me make a decision," Oprah told him. "Should I give up school and radio?"

Dr. Cox talked later about his response. Students came to college so they would be able to make decisions about their future, he reminded Oprah. His next action gave Oprah the answer, and the confidence she wanted. Dr. Cox handed her a dime to telephone the television station.

Oprah Winfrey, a college student, became the first woman TV co-anchor in Nashville. Of course, she was the first black co-anchor in that city. In addition, she continued her studies at TSU.

Oprah was hired to do the weekend news. In many ways the television assignment was quite different from her radio experience. On television her every movement would be broadcast.

She had to master the mechanics of getting ready for the newscast. Harry Chapman, Oprah's co-anchor, was helpful here. They usually began their work in the early afternoon. They talked with an assignment editor to discuss what stories they might cover that day. Would it be a political event? A press conference? A tragic fire? An accident? Oprah, Chapman, and the assignment editor decided which newsperson would cover each event selected.

From a local television personality, Oprah Winfrey skyrocketed to fame and received the Broadcaster of the Year award.

Oprah Winfrey now took on the role of reporter as well as newscaster. The trend in local news reporting was to have reporters broadcast the story they had actually covered. When Oprah went out to cover a story, she usually took a cameraman to record pictures. Whatever the nature of the story, Oprah was sure to become emotionally involved. She did more than probe. She showed empathy, especially if she covered a story that revolved around a tragic occurrence.

Returning to the television studio, Oprah prepared the script for the stories she would report that evening. She had to learn the art of writing scripts for television. She and her co-anchor decided which would be the lead story, and the sequence of the other news events. National as well as local news had to be considered.

It was exciting work. For someone as outgoing and as brash as Oprah, it was her cup of tea. There was one part of her work, however, that she could never completely adjust to. It was downright difficult for her to read the script exactly as she had written it when she went on the air. She was too creative. If she suddenly thought of a way to make the news story more interesting to listeners, she would change the wording. Her keen interest in people, and the understanding manner in which she questioned them about what happened, seemed unusual in a person her age. It gave a humanistic quality to her reporting. This made her popular. The trend was to have local TV news reporters come across as likeable human beings.

By six o'clock in the afternoon, Oprah and her co-anchor had to have every part of the program in place. They took seats in their assigned studio. The cameras were in position; cameramen, wearing earphones, waited for signals from the director in the control room. The studio lights were turned brighter. From the control room, the director gave a cue to the floor manager, who alerted everyone in the studio: "Stand by!"

Oprah Winfrey faced her public. If she made a mistake, she did not brood over it. She learned from the mistake and moved on.

After the six o'clock newscast, Oprah's busy day continued. She ate a hurried snack, then began preparing the script for the ten o'clock news.

Along with this lively schedule of a reporter-anchor, Oprah had to keep up her college studies. That took some doing. Luckily, each segment of her life supported another. Her studies and performance in speech and drama gave her added poise and confidence in broadcasting. On the other hand, her television experience provided practical application for her studies.

To Nashville's credit, the sight of a black, female reporter on Channel 5 caused relatively few negative responses. Chris Clark remembered how the TV station kept track of calls. He recalled only one negative call, and that, he said, was from a crank. At first some viewers voiced skepticism about the ability of such a young person. Oprah's talents and charisma soon won them over.

Vernon Winfrey supported his daughter. He may have had doubts about her moving away from a teaching career, but he did not discourage her from turning to television. There were some matters he was adamant about, however. He insisted that she get rest, and protect her health. Also, he was unyielding in the demand that she safeguard her reputation. This all boiled down to a continuing curfew for Oprah.

Oprah's father was not swayed by the fact that his daughter was making money, and that she was steadily becoming more famous as a television star. She was still a college student. She was under the protection of his household. She was his beloved daughter, still under his guidance. Her welfare was dear to him.

In 1976 Oprah Winfrey completed her studies at Tennessee State University. Technically, her coursework was still incomplete. Her hours had been so packed with television and community

Tennessee State University administration building, Nashville, Tennessee.

commitments, she did not complete her senior class project. The college held up the conferring of her degree.

With college classes over, Oprah could give full time to her television career. Her work at WTVF was changed to a full-time position. Her popularity assured a large viewing audience. Yet, the time had come for a change. Oprah knew this. As long as she stayed in Nashville, she felt she would never stretch her wings to their full power. She wanted to fly — as high as her wings would take her.

Her admirers read about her decision to make a change in *The Nashville Banner*. Oprah Winfrey was leaving WTVF — Channel 5. She was leaving Nashville. Oprah had accepted a position at WJZ-TV, Channel 13 in Baltimore, Maryland.

The salary offer was far higher than the money she was making. More important, though, Baltimore ranked among the top ten largest cities in the United States. Though the population was dropping, it was still nearly double Nashville's. A port city, near to the nation's capital, and with commuter trains to Philadelphia and New York, Baltimore seemed a perfect location for a talented woman with aspirations of becoming a force in the mushrooming television industry.

Oprah Winfrey was taking a gamble. She recognized that fact. But any move in life could be considered a gamble. Oprah needed a larger city with more chance to make new choices, meet new people, explore new possibilities — and then perhaps move on.

The staff of WTVF accepted Oprah's leaving with grace. They assured her that she could come back if the new job did not suit her.

The community of Nashville faced a loss. Admiring fans told Oprah how sad they were to see her leave.

Chris Clark at WTVF spoke words that described the sentiment of countless Nashville citizens. "She is a tremendously talented person. We hate to lose her."

For the first time in her life, Oprah Gail Winfrey would be completely on her own.

8

Talking in Baltimore

"What's an Oprah?" demanded the Baltimore billboards provocatively. Station WJZ-TV, an American Broadcasting Company (ABC) outlet, used the promotional technique to advertise a coming attraction. Naturally, the people of Baltimore became curious. Who was this Oprah coming to their city, they wondered.

Oprah Gail Winfrey was about to begin another cycle in her amazing life. She arrived in Baltimore in June, 1976. She was on her own. There would be no Daddy to set rules or give advice. She was independent—and in one of the most exciting cities in the United States. Oprah resolved to carve a niche for herself in the place known as "Charm City."

Still, for the first few days, all by herself in the big city, Oprah was lonely. One night she telephoned her Daddy and burst into tears. After a long chat with him she felt better. And then her "take-charge" personality took over.

Oprah looked for a place to stay. At first she chose a beautiful apartment in Columbia, a modern development in nearby Howard County, within easy commuting distance of Baltimore City. The trees and flowers reminded her of Nashville. Later she moved closer to her work, renting a two-bedroom apartment in Cross Keys, a modern complex not far from the WJZ-TV studios. The Cross Keys development offered an inn with excellent dining facilities. It also included a shopping section with stores that featured fashionable clothing. Landscaped trees and plants gave Cross Keys an atmosphere of suburban greenery, and the track at nearby Polytechnic High School was convenient for Oprah to jog several times a week.

At WJZ-TV, Channel 13, Oprah stepped into what was considered a "plum" position. She was hired as co-anchor with Jerry Turner, the most popular television newscaster in the city. For many Baltimore viewers, Jerry Turner was more popular than any of the national newscasters. As Bill Carter, the *Baltimore Sun* TV critic put it, "In the language of the television business, Jerry Turner owned the Baltimore market." Some critics named Turner the best local news anchor in the United States. He was more. He was tall, slender, silver-haired, and suave. And he was likeable. Citizens in Baltimore and most of the state of Maryland were saying, "Jerry Turner is a nice guy." He attended endless local functions, especially the ones to raise money for charitable causes. A trained musician, he could take over the baton and conduct the Baltimore Symphony during a fundraising telethon.

It was with this giant of newscasting that Oprah Winfrey was cast as co-anchor. She was only twenty-two years old. This girl from Tennessee had confidence, however, and she tackled the job with her usual gusto.

Television stations were changing the local news programming from thirty minutes to one hour. This was considered too long a span for one newscaster. In keeping with the trend to give more visibility to women and to black people, the anchor teams were often teaming a white man and a black woman.

The manager of WJZ-TV had to make changes before airing the new hour-long format. During the waiting period Oprah was given an assignment that helped her learn more about Baltimore City. Channel 13 planned a series of programs that explored the diverse neighborhoods, each so different in character, that made Baltimore unique. By the time Oprah finished the research and programming, the same thing had happened to her that had changed the first, sometimes negative, impression of others who came to work in the city: Baltimore charmed her. Oprah learned the fascinating history of how the city developed.

Baltimore was founded in 1729. Located on the great Patapsco River, it rapidly developed into a port city. Ships from many countries could bring their cargoes up the Chesapeake Bay and into Baltimore's harbor on the Patapsco. The city became a shipping, industrial, and manufacturing center.

The growing industries attracted people from many countries

Oprah Winfrey and Jerry Turner, co-anchoring the evening news on WJZ-TV Channel 13 in Baltimore, Maryland.

of the world. They came by ship and settled in various sections of the city. Immigrants tended to settle in communities according to their nationalities. Over the years, as these communities evolved, each neighborhood retained the ethnic characteristics of the group that had settled there — Italian, Irish, Polish, Czechoslovak, German, Greek, or African American. Every year, at a giant city fair, varied Baltimore communities take pride in displaying reminders of their ethnic heritage — foods, arts and crafts, music, and dancing.

Gradually, Oprah Winfrey began to understand why Baltimore was called "Charm City."

Her problem in Charm City arose partly from her on-air image and interaction with Jerry Turner. She admitted that she felt intimidated. She had to change the style of newscasting that had made her a hit in Nashville. She preferred to read the news in a spontaneous manner, rather than perfecting the reading of it beforehand. She did not easily conform to the rule of reading a script exactly as written. The major problem, however, was the difficulty in establishing her own identity while teamed with such a giant of newscasting. Oprah admitted that she was not as effective as she could be.

Another problem for Oprah, she confessed, was her approach to news gathering. As a journalist, she found it difficult to separate her emotions completely from the stories she covered, especially stories dealing with personal loss. "I'd have to fight back the tears if a story was too sad," she admitted.

One day Oprah was sent to interview a woman who had lost her home in a fire. At the scene, the woman, weeping hysterically, told Oprah that the seven children had all died in the blaze. When Oprah heard this news she began to cry too. At the TV station, she pleaded that the interview was too sad to show. It was shown anyway. At the end, Oprah apologized to the woman and to the viewers.

Oprah remained a co-anchor until the spring of 1977. On the

first day of April the management officials at Channel 13 called her in and broke the news. They were relieving her of her job as co-anchor with Jerry Turner.

Oprah accepted the news gracefully. She was not fired; she was still under contract. So the station had to find something to do with her.

First, an assistant news director hit upon what he considered a brilliant plan. Oprah's looks needed to be changed, he reasoned. On television in the 1970s, the appearance as well as the voice determined to a great degree the response from viewers.

One morning, this critic reminded Oprah of the things about her physical features that were wrong. He did not mince words, as Oprah later recalled — making light, as usual, her misadventures. "Your hair's too long. It's too thick. Your eyes are too far apart. Your nose is too wide. Your chin is too wide. And you need to do something about it."

For a brief time, Oprah was crestfallen. She had won top honors in beauty contests. Now she was being told that her features were all wrong.

The news director had a plan of action. Oprah would be sent to an expensive beauty salon in New York. They could do wonders for her, he promised.

Oprah obliged her bosses and traveled to New York's Manhattan for a consultation by a makeup artist. He gave her tips on makeup for her face.

Oprah's next stop was to a hair salon. She later described it as "a very chichi-pooh-pooh French salon." After examining her hair, the experts discussed what they would do, speaking in French. After the discussion, they began to work on Oprah's hair. Since her hair is thick and heavy, the experts used chemicals to straighten it out. They also let the chemicals stay on for extra minutes. Later Oprah described that she acted like a "mouseburger" and sat there while her scalp was "burning off."

Oprah returned to Baltimore, her hair much thinner. It was also falling out. Each day more was gone, until she was nearly bald. Oprah described her head as "billiard-ball bald."

It was during this anxious time, Oprah confessed later, that she went through a period of self-discovery. She found reasons for appreciating her own worth other than the way she looked.

There was more make-over in store for Oprah Winfrey. The

Oprah as a young reporter in Baltimore, Maryland.

assistant director did not particularly like her style of speaking. Next, Oprah was sent to a speech coach in New York. The discerning coach not only worked with her on speech but on attitude as well. You will never make it in broadcasting, the coach advised her, until you learn to stand up to the bosses when they make decisions you know are not the best ones for you.

What would they do with an Oprah? A new station manager took over at WJZ-TV. He knew exactly what to do with her. He tapped Oprah to co-host a new morning show called *People Are Talking*. The person picked as the other host was Richard Scher, a native of Baltimore. Older than Oprah, Scher had years of broadcasting experience. He was also calm and understanding.

Oprah Winfrey and Richard Scher made a championship team. The format suited Oprah well. She enjoyed talking and she liked to meet people.

The public response to the first show would be crucial. Oprah knew *People Are Talking* was scheduled for a time slot opposite *The Phil Donahue Show*, syndicated from Chicago.

People Are Talking needed a successful opening show to begin with a high rating. Guests for this premiere show included members of the cast of *All My Children*, the popular daytime soap opera.

The new team worked. Richard Sher and Oprah Winfrey clicked with the public. Oprah showed the relief she felt after the successful first show. "This is it," she said. "I've found out what I was *meant* to do. This is what I was *born* for. This is like *breathing*!"

Viewers sensed Oprah Winfrey's exuberance; they said they liked her down-to-earth realness. They admired Richard Sher's easygoing likeable style. *People Are Talking* gained a wide viewing audience rapidly. In a short period it had more viewers than *The Phil Donahue Show*.

Oprah Winfrey had found success in Baltimore. She also found romance. Her first steady boyfriend was a reporter who remained devoted to her. "That man loved me even when I was bald," she reminisced later. Oprah called the friendship a "fun romance."

Her other romance was a topsy-turvy, on-and-off experience. When it ended, Oprah stayed in a state of depression for a long time. Finally, after weeks of worrying, she realized what had happened to her. In later years she shared the discovery with other women who had experienced "emotional abuse." She said, "I had given this man power over my life. And I will never, never—as long as I am black!—give up my power to another person."

Oprah discovered her own power to help other people solve their problems through the *People Are Talking* show. She learned to ask questions ordinary people would ask. She and Richard Sher tried to find guests who faced problems or experiences interesting to home viewers. They shaped the program so that viewers would grow in some measure by listening to the advice given by guests on the show.

Oprah and Richard were not only compatable co-hosts. They were good friends off the air. Often, on weekends, she would jog to the Sher home and have breakfast with his family.

Oprah's love for acting stayed with her through the years. In 1983 she had her first experience in acting for a nationwide television audience. She performed in one episode of *All My Children*, one of her favorite "soaps." Even though she had a minor role, she enjoyed every minute of the taping in New York City, and she returned to Baltimore dreaming of having a major acting role someday.

People Are Talking continued to get higher and higher ratings. Locally, it maintained a higher rating than *The Phil Donahue Show.*

In Baltimore, Oprah continued with the type of community involvement that she had pursued in Nashville. She frequently visited schools and talked with students. She encouraged them to stay in school and take advantage of opportunities to learn. She spoke in churches and at colleges, and before huge crowds for civic events. At one time her schedule included as many as six speaking appointments each week.

Oprah went out of her way to talk with teenage groups, especially those considered underprivileged. On more than one occasion she told a group, "I was like a lot of you." Oprah urged young people to read, and learn to speak well. She reminded them that they are "already ten paces behind" if they lack education and the ability to speak well.

An associate producer of *People Are Talking*, Debra (Debbie) DiMaio, began looking around for another job. As part of her credentials, she sent tapes of shows she had produced. When the station managers saw Debbie's productions, they naturally saw Oprah in action. Debbie was hired by WLS-TV, the ABC affiliate in Chicago. She became producer of the talk show *A.M. Chicago*.

When Dennis Swanson, the WLS-TV station manager, examined Miss DiMaio's audition reel, he took note of Oprah Winfrey on *People Are Talking*. He decided that he wanted to meet this young lady one day. The chance came soon.

Not long after Debbie DiMaio took over as producer of *A.M. Chicago*, the host of the show, Rob Weller, resigned. This meant that an assortment of guest hosts had to fill in until a permanent replacement could be found. In the meantime, many of the show's faithful fans switched to watching Phil Donahue, also slotted at the 9:00 A.M. viewing time.

Both Debbie DiMaio and Dennis Swanson remembered that Oprah Winfrey's *People Are Talking* had out-rated Donahue in the Baltimore market. Could she do the same in Chicago? they wondered. They decided it was worth the try. The *A.M. Chicago* show had to have a drastic change of image if it was to survive.

Dennis Swanson sent for Oprah Winfrey to come to Chicago for an interview. Oprah's sense of timing let her know that the moment had come to expand her ever-widening world, to move on. She planned a trip to Chicago.

9

At Home in Chicago

"I knew I belonged here."

This was how Oprah Winfrey described her feeling when she arrived in Chicago. In an interview she talked about her excitement. "I'll tell you this, my first day in Chicago, September fourth, 1983, I set foot in this city, and just walking down the street, it was like roots, like the motherland."

Oprah came to Chicago for her interview with Dennis Swanson, vice president and general sales manager of WLS-TV. "You can forget it!" — that was her first reaction, she told *Ebony*. "They're not going to put a black woman on at nine in the morning — not in Chicago, not on prime-time television."

Vernon Winfrey's daughter did not give up easily, however. In all her years of working, she had never had to go out to seek a position. The people responsible for hiring had come to her. This time she had put together a résumé, a summary of her accomplishments. For her work, this included putting together tapes of successful shows. With her résumé, including an audition reel made up of samplings of her work, Oprah checked into a Chicago hotel.

She decided to study the show *A.M. Chicago* before going to talk with Dennis Swanson. She turned on the television set in her hotel room and, as she watched, she made mental notes of changes that could make the program more interesting.

By the time Oprah sat in an office to talk with the WLS-TV executives, she radiated confidence. Oprah cleared the air with one key question. She talked about this question in a speech she gave later before the Chicago Broadcast Ad Club. "Well," she told Swanson, "You know I'm black."

Dennis Swanson answered without hesitation. He did not care what color she was, he told her. "You can be green. All we want to do is win. I'm in the business of winning, and I want you to go for it."

The WLS executive board hired Oprah Winfrey as the new host of *A.M. Chicago*. "Dynamic" was how they described her.

As elated as she was over the new job, Oprah hated to leave the good friends and colleagues she had learned to love and respect. But her zest for climbing new mountains took her to what was then the nation's second largest city. Most of her life she had been taking on challenges and kicking aside obstacles. Chicago would be her biggest challenge.

She faced the odds against her with honesty. Success would depend upon the future rating of the show; for the moment, with its very low TV rating, the show was failing badly. If people did not watch a TV show, low ratings spelled disaster. Advertisers tried to choose popular programs to publicize their commercials. The larger the viewing audience, the higher the potential buying power for items shown during commercial breaks.

In Oprah's case, there was an even stiffer challenge: Phil Donahue's talk show came on at the same time as *A.M. Chicago*, on a different station. And Chicagoans loved Donahue. The ratings for this show were consistently high in the city.

Many people did not give Oprah the ghost of a chance. The

viewing audience for *A.M. Chicago* would be largely white, and mainly housewives. These viewers could get their families off to work and school, then relax to watch a 9:00 A.M. talk show. Would they watch Oprah?

In past years, Chicago had had the reputation of a city with serious racial problems. Many suburban neighborhoods excluded African Americans from buying or renting homes. Slum neighborhoods were overcrowded.

In 1966, Dr. Martin Luther King, Jr. had begun a crusade to dramatize the need for changes in cities such as Chicago. He moved his wife and young children to that city and lived in a ghetto neighborhood. This focused national attention upon the problems faced by the poor and the minorities in large northern cities. Dr.

Oprah weaves her magic and wins the hearts of Chicago television viewers.

King planned interracial marches into segregated neighborhoods to demonstrate the need for city officials to work actively for better housing, jobs, and more harmonious race relations.

At first, diehard segregationists resisted. Peaceful interracial marchers were pelted with stones and debris. In one neighborhood Dr. King was knocked to his knees by a rock.

Finally, Chicago mayor Richard Daley met with Dr. King and local leaders to negotiate improvements in housing, job opportunities, and other spheres.

Over the seven years since, dramatic improvements had been made. Jesse Jackson, one of Dr. King's staff members, had supervised a successful program called "Operation Breadbasket." Black customers were being encouraged to buy from businesses that used fair hiring practices. Housing conditions had improved. Many formerly segregated neighborhoods were now interracial. And Chicago, like many cities across America, had become accustomed to seeing dark-skinned people working all over town.

In 1983 there was still racial friction and bigotry, but these were balanced by signs of tremendous change. A few months before Oprah arrived, Chicago elected Harold Washington as mayor. He was black. Several other top city officials were also black.

Outmoded attitudes and practices were slowly changing in Chicago. Racism still existed. But in her usual aggressive way, Oprah Winfrey set out to win over all segments of Chicago, the "Windy City."

The salary offered her was a huge incentive, coupled with her personal pride. The salary was reported to be more than $200,000 dollars a year. In addition, Oprah's agent, at that time Ron Shapiro, saw to it that she also got a four-year unbreakable contract.

Despite the salary and the publicity, Oprah's eyes welled with tears when the time came to leave Baltimore. During her seven years in the city, as she said herself, she had grown up at WJZ-TV, where she felt nurtured and cared for.

Before Oprah left Baltimore, co-workers at Station WJZ-TV made a compilation of film clips to show some of her most successful moments from *People Are Talking*. The clips reminded Oprah, as well as her viewing audience, just how much the girl from Tennessee had matured during her Baltimore years.

So Oprah Winfrey left Baltimore for Chicago. She was on her way, and for her, the arrows pointed upward. In her words, she was "released into the universe."

The city Oprah set out to win over was the third largest television market in the country. She knew she could not compete

Oprah orchestrates her guest panel of Robin Williams, Billy Crystal, Dudley Moore, and John Larroquette to interact with the audience and keep her talk show lively.

by trying to imitate another existing talk show. Her surest way, Oprah decided, was to put the stamp of her own personality upon the traditional talk-show format.

Dennis Swanson gave her free rein to shape the *A.M. Chicago* show. When people asked him why he hired her, he answered, "She was the best and I wanted the best." Oprah, he said, "is the same person on camera as she is off camera. She's a bundle of energy and fun to be around."

In early 1984, Oprah Winfrey combined three ingredients — energy, fun, and naturalness — to develop the style of her *A.M. Chicago* shows. She had a lot going for her. She also had some things that could draw her back, if she let them. In an industry that glorified slim, trim bodies, she could be described as fat. She had put on weight during the Baltimore years. The weight was well distributed, though, and at about five feet six inches, she carried herself with such regal assurance that size did not seem to matter — except to those who enjoyed gossiping about it, all the while loving every inch of Oprah.

Oprah confessed one reason for her steady weight gain. "Everybody kept telling me that it was going to be impossible to succeed because I was going into Phil Donahue's home town. So, you know, I'd eat and eat." And since television usually tends to make people look larger than they are, it made Oprah look even heavier than she was.

But, such is human nature, this all seemed to endear her to Chicago viewers. Most of them were not thin-thighed, pencil-slim models. They felt comfortable with Oprah. Her buoyant personality seemed to reach out to viewers. And from the opening show, Oprah came across as enjoying the studio audience. Some television stars may be intimidated by the mike; Oprah loved it. One TV critic said, "the mike embraces her." With her personal, down-home style she began to win over a large segment of Chicago viewers, and she even won over many who were at first determined to resist her. She did this by just being — Oprah.

With assistance from the group of young people who made up her staff, she tried to select subjects for each show that she felt people would really want to know more about. As her viewing audience got to know her better, they began telephoning the studio with ideas for future subjects to be discussed on the show.

To the amazement of television critics, Oprah and *A.M. Chicago* kept increasing in popularity. The city and much of the nation discovered the talent and the adventurous spirit of Oprah Winfrey. They wondered what she would do next.

10

The Color Purple

Oprah's fast-paced schedule always included time to read exciting books. During the summer of 1982 she read reviews of a novel and immediately called one of the bookstores she patronized. She asked to be called the minute the fiction reached the Baltimore bookstores.

She stood in line to buy several copies. She became so excited over the novel that she wanted her friends to read it also. As Oprah told Lou Cedrone of the *Baltimore Sun*, "If you got married, you got a copy. If you had a baby, you got a copy. If you got divorced, you got a copy. I thought it one of the best books I had ever read." She could identify with the characters in *The Color Purple*. She told friends, "There is magic in that book."

The emotionally powerful novel by Alice Walker, published by Harcourt Brace Jovanovich, sold millions of copies. The book's author is as fascinating as some of the characters she creates.

The Color Purple tells the story of a poor black girl growing up in rural Georgia during the early days of this century. Alice Walker understood the poverty and problems of sharecropping families in the rural South. She was born in Eatontan, Georgia, in 1944, the youngest of eight children. While a very young girl, one of her brothers accidentally shot her with a BB gun and put out one eye. She later attended Spelman College in Atlanta, Georgia on a scholarship for disabled students.

Before writing *The Color Purple*, Alice Walker had become well established as an author. Her publishing successes included *Meridian, Good Night Willie Lee, I'll See You in the Morning*, and other bestsellers.

The Color Purple immediately captured wide acclaim and won Alice Walker the 1983 Pulitzer Prize for fiction. The Pulitzer Prizes were established by Joseph Pulitzer (1847–1911), one of America's greatest journalists and newspaper owners.

Joseph Pulitzer left a fortune and directed that part of the funds be used to establish prizes in various departments of journalism and literature. One of the annual prizes is awarded for distinguished fiction published in book form during the year by an American author, preferably dealing with American life.

Gwendolyn Brooks, the poet and novelist, became the first African American to have her work honored by the coveted prize. *Annie Allen*, her volume of poetry, won the 1950 Pulitzer Prize for poetry.

Alice Walker became the second member of her race to receive it, and the first to win in the fiction category. The author, and her winning fiction, *The Color Purple*, joined a distinguished list of winners including *Gone With the Wind* by Margaret Mitchell; *The Old Man and the Sea* by Ernest Hemingway; *To Kill a Mockingbird* by Harper Lee; and other classics of American literature.

Alice Walker's novel is told chiefly through letters exchanged between two sisters. The letters are written by poorly schooled folk in Georgia. Some are written by Celie, the central character. Others are written by Celie's sister, Nettie, who has run away from home to keep from being abused by their cruel stepfather. The stepfather hides the letters written by Nettie, so that for years Celie does not know what has happened to her beloved sister. In her harsh and lonely existence, Celie shares her thoughts with God. She addresses her letters, "Dear God."

In her letters, Celie reveals how she is sexually molested by her stepfather at age fourteen, and bears two children. The children are sold by the cruel stepfather. Celie is later forced to marry a widower whom she addresses as Mister, and who treats her as his slave.

Mister becomes increasingly more insulting as years pass. He

Alice Walker, contemporary of Oprah Winfrey, and author of the Pulitzer Prize winning novel, *The Color Purple*.

even brings his girlfriend Shug (short for Sugar) to live in their home with them. Through it all, Celie exhibits the indomitable will of the human spirit to survive. And—surprisingly—it is Shug who helps foster Celie's sense of strong womanhood. Another person who helps Celie gain more independence is Sofia, the robust, proud, tough wife of Mister's son, named Harpo.

The Color Purple would make a tremendous movie, Steven Spielberg decided. This gifted director had won honors for movies such as *Raiders of the Lost Ark* and *E.T.* Spielberg teamed with a musical genius, Quincy Jones, who worked as co-producer of the film.

Steven Spielberg and Quincy Jones began scouting for actors to play the various roles in *The Color Purple*. There were many black actors who wanted to be considered. Whoopi Goldberg joked that she would have played the part of the dirt just to be in the movie.

Oprah, who still nurtured her strong love for acting, had the same strong urge to be a part of the project. "If they would just let me carry water to the set, I'd be ecstatic," she said.

It was Quincy Jones who chose Oprah. The musician arrived in Chicago for a brief stopover. He came to testify in a court case involving Michael Jackson's writing of a song.

The co-producer of *The Color Purple* checked into a Chicago hotel. He turned on the television in his room to relax while he ate breakfast. By chance he tuned to *A.M. Chicago*. Oprah's vibrant personality filled the television screen. Quincy Jones told later how he watched her moving with such assurance among the studio guests. He decided, "That's Sofia!" He immediately called the casting director for the movie.

The wheels started spinning. Oprah was invited to do a screen test and script reading. Later she went for auditions in Hollywood for more tests with actor Willard Pugh, who tried out to play the part of Harpo. One day in the middle of testing the thought hit Oprah: Harpo is Oprah spelled backward. For her, she confessed, this was a sign that she was meant to play the role of Sofia.

And so she was: Steven Spielberg agreed that Oprah could define the character of Sofia. Willard Pugh accepted the role of Harpo, Sofia's husband.

The moment the news reached Oprah, she said later, was the greatest moment of her life. "Maybe the day I was born was the greater, but I can't remember that experience." This was confirmation of her feeling that she had been an actress in spirit all her life.

There was still the problem of Oprah's contract with WLS-TV to do the *A.M. Chicago* program every morning. The problem was solved by using guest hosts for some programs. For other days, the program included reruns of some of Oprah's most popular shows.

The filming of *The Color Purple* took place in Monroe, North Carolina.

Oprah could scarcely contain her excitement. "I feel very blessed that I was discovered by Quincy Jones and that he also had this vision to know that I could do it," she said later.

Oprah worked hard to actually become Sofia in the film. While the film was being made, she could happily forget about dieting. The character she depicted was supposed to be a stout woman, tough, strong and independent. And ever since high-school days, Oprah had highlighted the strength of black women in her dramatic skits for schools and community programs.

Oprah could understand the unbreakable will of Sofia, the headstrong rural woman whose part she was playing. As she put it, "Sofia represents a legacy of black women and the bridges that I've crossed to get where I am. She's a combination to me of Sojourner Truth and Harriet Tubman and Fannie Lou Hamer, and grandmothers and aunts of mine and other black women who have gone unnamed but who represent a significant part of our history."

Oprah used her feeling for these women to shape an

unforgettable character. She had portrayed the feisty Sojourner Truth in dramatic productions and she knew Sojourner's spirit well. Harriet Tubman was another woman who lived during the period of slavery. She fearlessly guided runaway slaves away from plantations, traveling by night until they could reach sympathetic freedom fighters, or abolitionists (people who actively opposed slavery) who helped them. Harriet knew that she ran the risk of being sold back into slavery, or killed. Yet she never gave up the dangerous work. And she refused to let the runaway slaves become fearful and turn back. A huge reward was offered for her capture "dead or alive." Harriet scorned it and went back south again and again to lead people out of slavery. She earned the name Moses, for the Biblical hero who likewise led his people out of bondage.

Fannie Lou Hamer, another of Oprah's "legacy of black women," was a heroine of a modern freedom movement inspired by Dr. Martin Luther King, Jr. Fannie Lou grew up poor, the last of twenty children in a sharecropping family. She recalled how hard they worked, and how hungry they were. At the age of six, Fannie Lou was picking sixty pounds of cotton a day. She later married and lived as a worker on a white-owned plantation.

Fannie Hamer was inspired by the hundreds of black and white college students who came to Mississippi in the 1960s to help black people win their constitutional right to vote. One day she went to register, only to be given an ultimatum by her boss: withdraw her name or be fired. Fannie Lou's blunt answer showed her courage. "I didn't register for you, I tried to register for myself."

So Fannie Lou Hamer left sharecropping and became a part of the nonviolent freedom movement. She was jailed, beaten, threatened, but none of it broke her spirit. Instead, she grew stronger.

In August 1964 she was one of the black Freedom Delegates who challenged the seating of all-white Mississippi delegations at the Democratic Conventions. Freedom Delegates were people who supported equal rights for everyone. The black delegates were not seated in 1964, but they won the admiration of a sympathizing world as their actions were seen on television. The cameras caught the unyielding determination on Fannie Hamer's face.

She was a stout women, with luminous dark eyes and heavy black hair. When she sang freedom songs in her strong emotional voice, they seemed to open her soul. She raised her powerful voice and led freedom songs right on the convention floor. And when the black Mississippi delegation was offered two token seats, it was her reply that people remembered: "We didn't come all this way for no two seats."

"I had Fannie Lou Hamer in the back of my head," Oprah revealed. Her portrayal of the role of Sofia, was strong and convincing, and brought out Sofia's determination.

In December 1985 Oprah went to New York for the premiere of *The Color Purple*. As soon as the film was released, the lines formed at theaters across the country. Publicity by word of mouth kept the crowds coming. And at each showing, the sound of sniffling could be heard as people wept. Audiences had as many white as black patrons. The message of Alice Walker's novel is not only for black people, it is universal. The majority of critics had high praise for Oprah's acting.

All movie critics did not agree with the enthusiasm of movie patrons about the movie, however. Some were downright harsh on Spielberg for the manner in which they felt he had diluted parts of the powerful novel, including Sofia's confrontation with the white mayor and his wife. Even so, critics admitted that the unique construction of the story made the transition to film quite difficult.

The harsh criticisms seemed to only increase people's curiosity to see *The Color Purple*.

The most outspoken critics of all were black men. They mounted a solid protest over the manner in which black males were presented. Explanations that it was only *one* story about *one* family did not put down the outcry. In city after city, there were public discussions in churches, libraries, and other meeting places to air the debate.

Oprah offered a subduing reminder for everyone. "I tell people that the movie is not for or against men." she said. "*The Color Purple* is a novel about women." Other perceptive critics extended this idea. The story, they argued, is about the bonding and sisterhood of women. It is also about the kinship of native Africans and African Americans. Above all, the story underscores the healing and redemptive power of love.

When Academy Awards nominations were announced for 1985 films, *The Color Purple* was placed in the running for eleven of the prestigious Oscars. This included nomination for best picture.

Oprah's strong sense-of-self helps her to dramatize Sofia's struggle for survival of the human spirit.

Whoopi Goldberg as Celie was nominated for best actress. And not one but two people were nominated for best supporting actress — Margaret Avery as Shug, and Oprah Winfrey as Sofia.

Yes, Oprah Winfrey — in her very first film. When Vernon Winfrey learned of it, he went to see the movie for himself. This was no small matter. Oprah's father confessed that he had not been to see a movie in twenty-five years.

The month before the Oscars ceremonies, Oprah won another honor that meant a great deal to her. She flew to Baltimore to accept the city's first annual "Homecoming Celebrity Award." The Chicago talk-show hostess was ecstatic as she breezed into Joseph Meyerhoff Hall dressed in furs. She kissed Baltimore's Mayor William Donald Schaefer and the two stood hamming it up, obviously delighted to see each other. Oprah had more hugs and kisses for Richard Sher, her former co-host, when she went on stage. Sher hosted the evening's event, which was sponsored by the "Baltimore Is Best" program of the Mayor's Office.

The evening in Baltimore was a refreshing visit for the Academy Award nominee. She was back in the city that helped to shape her career. Floraine Applefield, executive director of the Baltimore Is Best program, summed up the city's affection for the honoree: "Ope, as we called her, was here for eight years and we watched her grow and we thought she was a star before she became a movie star."

Oprah was presented with an engraved tray and a charm bracelet by Mayor Schaefer and Floraine Applefield.

Following that whirlwind Baltimore trip, Oprah began preparations for the Academy Awards appearance. Getting ready is no small matter, especially if you expect to walk up to the stage and accept an Oscar with the world watching.

She had a designer fashion a special gown for the occasion. She refused to wear purple as some friends suggested, but chose instead a classy gown of ivory and gold, trimmed with beads. She bought expensive new shoes, earrings, and a bag, everything to complement the outfit.

For stars and others involved in *The Color Purple*, the news on Oscar night was astounding. Not a single one of the nominations won an Oscar. Not one! It was a complete shutout. Eleven nominations and not a single winner.

Why? Was it too much hype over Oprah's nomination? Criticisms? Too many black stars nominated? Perhaps a bit of jealousy or dislike for Steven Spielberg? The strong protest by so many black men over the film? It could have been a combination of all these factors. Nevertheless, despite the film's genuine popularity, it was practically ignored in the final selection.

Oprah, like the millions viewing the ceremonies, was stunned. She wasted short time over the matter, however. After all, she had been nominated — and for a first film role.

The real-life Sofia could not waste time on disappointments. Her life was moving too fast. Oprah Winfrey was ready for the next big challenge.

That challenge involved another movie. This one was based upon Richard Wright's novel, *Native Son*. Like Oprah, the world-acclaimed novelist was born in Mississippi but gained fame while he lived in Chicago.

Richard Wright was a close friend of Margaret Walker, whose poem, "For My People," was a favorite with Oprah. Wright's gripping stories exposed the social conditions that spawned the tragic lives of people forced to live in big-city slums. At the heart of the problem, he believed, was poverty — and also racism.

The black author felt the sting of poverty while growing up hungry in the Deep South, and during years of struggling in a Northern city to care for a crippled mother, he read books and hoped to become a writer. With help from the Federal Writers' Project set up during the Great Depression, he refined his creative skills and began writing novels to dramatize the causes of social problems. The main characters were black. Their problems were universal.

The central character of *Native Son* is Bigger Thomas, an impoverished, tortured young man whose rage against the barriers of racism contributes to his murder of a rich white girl. In the film version, Oprah plays the role of Bigger's mother, a woman exhausted from trying to keep her children fed and housed. Oprah actually "becomes" the poor woman, begging the mother of the murdered white girl, "Don't let them kill my boy. He's a poor boy." As the mother, Oprah cries out in pain at the idea that she and her other children would be put out on the streets with no place to go. Her powerful acting well conveys the feeling of desperation endured by poor families.

Even though *Native Son* did not enjoy great popularity in movie theaters, Oprah was praised by movie critics for her acting. Some people wondered whether she would again receive an Academy Award nomination. She did not win a nomination, but she was there at the Awards ceremonies, this time as a presenter.

The roles in *The Color Purple* and *Native Son* convinced Oprah Winfrey that at least a part of her future would be involved with movie production. These productions, she envisioned, would bring to the screen classic works by and about black people, thereby creating opportunities for talented black performers.

One of the truly happy occasions for Oprah during that eventful year of 1986 was her participation in the wedding of Maria Shriver. Maria is the daughter of Eunice Kennedy Shriver, sister of President John F. Kennedy. Oprah was more than just one of the four hundred and fifty guests, for Oprah and Maria had became close friends when the two young women were working at the same television station in Baltimore.

While family and friends assembled for the wedding, onlookers gathered outside the church to get a peek at the fairytale wedding. Some even climbed in trees.

Maria's groom was the well known Arnold Schwarzenegger, the muscular and handsome actor. Many in the crowd also pushed for a glimpse of Oprah Winfrey as she arrived wearing a fashionable flowing creation and dazzling the crowd with her magnetic smile.

Later, during the ceremonies, the guests inside St. Francis Xavier Roman Catholic Church listened enthralled as Oprah's expressive voice saluted the couple with the love sonnet written by Elizabeth Barrett Browning:

> How do I love thee? Let me count the ways.
> I love thee to the depth and breadth and height
> My soul can reach . . .
> . . . I love thee with the breath,
> Smiles, tears, of all my life! — and if God choose,
> I shall but love thee better after death.

11

The Toast of Talk

"This is my year!" Oprah said these words with confidence in 1986.

Her prediction was right on target. The year continued to be a happy period when the things she had worked hard for suddenly came together in a seemingly magical manner.

Events were swirling swiftly around the talk-show host. Her show had been expanded from thirty minutes to one hour. For several months national syndication operations had worked to get the rights to distribute the program to other cities. Oprah and her talk show had become so popular in Chicago that syndicators felt certain she would capture a large viewing audience in other big cities. Syndications, or associations of financial backers, bid for the rights to market TV shows to stations throughout the United States.

King World Productions, Inc., was one of these successful syndicators. One of their top-rated shows was *Wheel of Fortune*. King World negotiated a successful agreement with Oprah and Chicago's WLS-TV to distribute Oprah's show. In preparation for a national viewing audience, the name of the show was changed from *A.M. Chicago* to *The Oprah Winfrey Show*. The agreement called for WLS-TV to continue to produce the program. Through syndication, King World could sell the talk show to independent stations or networks. The contract called for Oprah to receive a percentage of the gross earnings. If the deal proved successful, she could make untold millions of dollars.

The national debut of *The Oprah Winfrey Show* was scheduled for September, 1986. In the months before that date, all parties concerned with the syndication began to publicize the upcoming event and create interest throughout the country.

The top executives of King World Productions knew that they had the making of a prosperous deal. One representative called it the hottest-selling show they ever handled. They made arrangements to show tapes of some of Oprah's Chicago talk shows

Oprah with top executives of King World Productions formalize plans for *The Oprah Winfrey Show*.

to spread interest in target cities. Television viewers in these cities liked what they saw, and stations began to bid on the right to air *The Oprah Winfrey Show*. It would emanate from Chicago. These TV executives knew that the majority of watchers of the daytime talk programs were women. Housewives were usually the family members who bought products advertised during commercial breaks. Therefore, a huge viewing audience meant fortunes in commercial advertisements.

Investors also knew that Oprah Winfrey had become well known internationally as Sofia in *The Color Purple*. Her Oscar nomination made her name and features even more familiar. With Oprah's growing popularity, scores of newspaper columnists, television critics, and magazine writers worked to keep her in the public eye.

Published accounts of Oprah's interviews, printed in magazines and newspapers, increased her popularity. Feature articles about her community involvements won other admirers. Many people who read these articles were amazed to learn of the problems Oprah had overcome during her earlier life. Stories of her life on a rural Mississippi farm, of never owning store-bought toys, of her rebellion against the social barriers that thwarted her talents during her early teens—these all seemed to make Oprah more real to everyday folk. Some entertainment stars seem to be so perfect that people fail to feel deep passion for them. As Richard Zogline put it that same year, in an article for *Time*, "People sense the realness." "She's very natural," added Lou Cedrone in the *Baltimore Sun*.

In city after city, viewers marked the September date and time when *The Oprah Winfrey Show* would be shown. It would be a first. Never before in America had a black woman hosted a national TV talk show. And nobody could mistake the star for any race but black. She was, as Oprah described herself, "a fudge brownie." She was a stunning "fudge"—intelligent, witty, sincere. Would that combination win over skeptics or viewers who might have a racist attitude? King World Productions bet both their money and reputation on Oprah's potential.

Extra publicity came from TV critics who began to pit Oprah's show against the national talk show hosted by Phil Donahue, now produced in New York. Oprah had outrated Donahue in Chicago. Critics questioned whether she could successfully compete against him on a national scale.

Home critics also formed their own views. Phil Donahue was billed as the "heavyweight." He had charted the course for the daytime talk show format, his admirers recalled. Also, to be realistic, he was a man, in an industry dominated by males. He was handsome. He was intelligent and articulate. And — he was white.

Oprah Winfrey was billed as the "challenger," trying for a share of the national viewing public. She had the same skills as Phil Donahue. As for prejudice, the Freedom Movement had altered the racial intolerance in most phases of American life. Viewers had become accustomed to seeing black faces on television in starring roles. Two of the top-rated stars were Bill Cosby in *The Cosby Show* and Bryant Gumbel on the early morning *Today Show*.

Oprah's admirers believed it was time for a black woman to take center stage in TV ratings. They admitted she was not pencil-slim like stereotypic television stars. In fact, Oprah was definitely overweight, with heavy thighs that she often made jokes about. Her admirers believed her size would make women feel more sympathetic toward her and more receptive to the thoughts she wanted to share with them.

As the date for Oprah's premiere show grew closer, American viewers waited with expectation. If the first show proved to be a success, this could well mean popularity for future programs. What surprises would Oprah's first national program feature? The public began to guess.

Oprah and her staff kept the topic a secret. The public could only speculate. Regular viewers of daytime talk shows believed that a big name personality would be featured. But who?

The guessing continued. Would Oprah bring on a movie idol? Or perhaps a popular politician? A sports hero? Someone universally admired? Mother Teresa? Quincy Jones? Steven Spielberg? Whoopi Goldberg? Michael Jackson?

By September, the beginning of a new season of television programming, at least one hundred thirty-eight cities had already contracted to receive *The Oprah Winfrey Show*. And the show's host was ready for these cities. "I feel as good as you can feel and still live," she said in happiness.

On Monday morning, September 8, national audiences heard the deep, rich voice that had won so many oratorical contests call out a greeting: "This is the Oprah Winfrey Show!" And there was the host, coming into American homes like a next-door neighbor dropping in for an hour's chat over a morning cup of coffee. Viewers saw the large eyes that danced with the joy of life, the luxuriant black hair, the trade-mark earrings, the all-embracing smile. National audiences got a taste of Oprah's wit as she moved among the studio guests, holding the hand microphone to let one after another speak their minds to the listening world. Always, though, it was Oprah who orchestrated the show. She was in conrol, ready to cut quickly to a commercial if she needed to regroup. There was no formal script. Characteristically, Oprah took cues from leads given by the featured guests and members of the studio audience. Oprah Winfrey likes her shows to come across as spontaneous, unpredictable, and fun to watch.

The topic for that first day of syndicated showing was one sure to draw viewers. It discussed the question, "How do you choose a mate?" The main guest was an author who had written a book on the subject of mate-catching. The book sold for ninety-five dollars! People who had bought the expensive publication came to talk about it.

For that day and the remainder of the week, Oprah held her own in the TV ratings. Even the tough television critics agreed that despite their differences in style, she was not overshadowed by Phil Donahue. Oprah's big plus, one critic acknowledged, was her ability to make studio guests as well as home viewers feel comfortable.

Oprah's biggest publicity agents were the people of all ages who watched her show. "Did you see Oprah today?" friends and coworkers would ask one another. Family members recalled high moments of favorite shows over local and long-distance telephones. They talked about what Oprah wore and what she said.

The syndication turned out to be a lucrative venture for Oprah. The December 1986 issue of *Variety* magazine called her contractual agreement a "WINFREY WHAMMO SYNDIE DEAL." The contract reportedly called for Oprah to get twenty-five percent of the gross earnings. Experts predicted she could earn more than thirty million dollars in a single season.

The contract Oprah signed made her one of the highest-paid stars in the television industry.

Oprah Winfrey summed up her phenomenal success with her customary verve: "I was like a hit album waiting to be released."

Growing success brought more fans and friends. "Everybody loves Oprah Winfrey" became a familiar saying. With this outpouring of affection from fans, however, there naturally came criticisms as well. Some came from African-American viewers. They said Oprah was partial to white guests, who usually made up the majority of the studio audiences. Oprah was accused of hugging white studio guests more than she hugged the guests of her own race. There were other viewers who saw the TV host as acting like a black "mammy" toward whites in the studio audience.

In a typical show of understanding, Oprah invited TV viewers who had sent in criticisms to be her guests for lunch one day. Many critics came, and they told her to her face why they disliked her. "I don't like the way you wear your hair," said one. "I don't like the clothes you wear," said another. "I don't like your earrings," came from a third. The litany of dislikes went on through lunch. Some of the luncheon guests said they just did not like Oprah "no way."

Oprah Winfrey had gained enough maturity and wisdom to understand human nature. She knew she would read one hundred letters telling her how much she was loved. Then she would come to one letter that ripped her to shreds for how she looked, or what she said or did during the show.

A number of critics felt that Oprah was treating the various serious problems brought up on her show too lightly. They believed that her hugs and kisses and tears were sometimes a bit too much.

Oprah Winfrey views her actions on a different level from such skeptics. Her work is a form of ministry, she says, — a chance to let people know that they are not alone with their problems. Her belief, she says, is that what most people need is courage to take charge of their own lives, to face their problems honestly and feel that they have the power to work for solutions. When viewers with personal problems listen and learn how others faced and dealt with similar situations, they begin to see life in more optimistic colors. Oprah Winfrey does not tailor her shows to avoid criticism. She shapes them to reach out and touch people — the ordinary people of this world.

A national audience was not the only big change in Oprah Winfrey's life. She moved into a new home. Oprah bought the place as a birthday present, she told friends. She had earlier made a promise to herself that by the time she reached the age of thirty-two, she would be a millionaire. She had made good on that promise. She rewarded herself with more glamorous living quarters.

Visitors to Oprah's lakeside condominium used impressive terms to describe its unique features: Posh! Gorgeous! Palatial! Lavish! Tasteful! Opulent! Wow!

The high-rise condominium was in a section with some of

Chicago's most expensive properties. Looking out from the large windows of her fifty-seventh-floor rooms, Oprah had a panoramic view of the city, and of the magnificent Lake Michigan. The condominium had once belonged to Evangeline Gouletas, wife of Hugh Carey, the former governor of New York State. The previous owner had designed the interior to suit her particular brand of lavish living.

Oprah Winfrey called in her interior decorator and styled the place to her own taste. Her old furnishings did not blend with the new home, the decorator decided, and for several months Oprah lived in a home nearly empty of furnishings except for the bedroom.

The redesigning was worth the wait. In the October 1988 issue of *Ebony*, the beauty of the rooms was shown in vivid color. Visitors who are privileged to visit the home praise Oprah's good taste.

The foyer is breathtaking, even before guests enter the main rooms. One visitor remarked with awe that the foyer seemed almost as large as some people's whole apartment. The floors are of marble. The walls display a gallery of paintings, many of them by African-American artists. The living room is furnished with sofa and chairs covered with white handwoven cotton. Tall green plants make a lovely contrast. Mounted before a living-room window is a telescope that can be used to get a full scenic view of Chicago's Lake Shore Drive. The white silk draperies are opened and closed by the touch of a button.

All the other rooms are just as beautifully decorated and just as restful in tone. A chandelier lights up Oprah's main clothes closet. In addition to Oprah's master bedroom there are two guest bedrooms. In the dining room, the color blue accentuates the windows, candlestick lights, and tapestry covering for the chairs. The master bedroom opens into a "media room" designed for listening and viewing. It is equipped with a huge television screen. A stereo system is built into the wall. Mounted on a side wall are some of Oprah's many awards. There are also framed magazine covers that feature her in a variety of poses. Oprah's picture on a magazine cover usually assures wide sales.

The library is fitted with custom-made shelves lined with books. The titles show Oprah's zest for reading. There are history books, biographies, fiction, books by African-American authors, religious works. A desk in the center of the room, with matching French chairs, provides a comfortable place for reading or writing. Music can be piped to any of the rooms by means of concealed speakers.

The new home was only one of the major additions to Oprah Winfrey's life. For months she had joked about waiting for "Mr. Right" to come along. She insisted that he must be tall, and that he must be spiritually grounded. Oprah often said in a joking manner that Mr. Right was on his way to her, but he must be walking from Africa. Sometimes she named some other faraway place instead of Africa.

Oprah discovered that her "Mr. Right" was there in Chicago. She was familiar with his name — Stedman Graham. She had seen him at civic and social functions.

One day Stedman Graham invited Oprah Winfrey to have dinner with him. Oprah turned him down. She had become wary of men who wanted to date her, knowing that some of them might be as interested in her growing fortune as in her friendship.

With Stedman Graham, there was something else that made her cautious. He was just so good-looking! He was tall, sleek, and personable.

Oprah Winfrey said she always kept in mind the admonition given by her mother, Vernita Lee: "Stay away from men who are prettier than you, or dumber."

Stedman Graham was thirty-six years old, six feet, six inches tall, and a former basketball star. At the time he became interested in Oprah, he was executive director of the non-profit program "Athletes Against Drugs." This program counseled youths against

Oprah Winfrey and Stedman Graham.

the dangers of substance abuse. Oprah knew that Stedman had been married and divorced, and that he was devoted to his young daughter, Wendy.

Stedman Graham turned out to be a determined man. He kept asking for a dinner date, and each time Oprah turned him down. What about lunch? he suggested — or maybe cocktails?

The answer was still the same. Her schedule was too busy, Oprah would say.

One day when Oprah's schedule had been unusually hectic, Stedman Graham telephoned just as she was preparing to leave her office. "This is the last time I'm going to ask," he told her. "Will you go out to dinner with me?"

Oprah surprised him. This time her answer was yes.

On the way to dinner that night Stedman impulsively stopped and bought her a bouquet of roses from someone selling flowers on the street. The thoughtful gesture told Oprah a lot about her dinner companion. So did his attentive attitude in listening to her as they ate. She had a chance to study his chiseled features and trim moustache from up close.

"Perrrr — fect!" Oprah later said of Stedman's looks. She elaborated: "I mean, you could bronze him and put him in an art gallery. He is six feet six of *terriffic!*"

Over the next weeks the friendship between Oprah Winfrey and Stedman Graham deepened into a closer relationship. Oprah and her "Mr. Right" could be seen walking hand in hand along Michigan Avenue, trying hard not to be noticed.

Stedman Graham had to become adjusted to the fact that when he accompanied one of the world's most popular TV stars, a crowd of people would gather and focus all their attention on *her*. Fortunately, he seemed secure enough to show patience and let Oprah's fans and celebrity seekers shower her with adulation.

Stedman Graham's actions showed Oprah he adopted a wise philosophy about his friendship with her. Both of them gained from each other. Because of his friendship with Oprah, his ideas gained greater scope, he said. On the other hand, Oprah had become more mature in action, and Stedman felt that he was responsible for part of that maturing. He said, "I always encourage her to be the best she can possibly be."

As the two spent more time together, Oprah learned more about Stedman Graham. He was born in Whitesboro, New Jersey, a town founded by his ancestors. He attended college at Hardin-Simmons University in Abilene, Texas, and became an outstanding basketball star, as well as a scholar. He went on to earn a master's degree in education from Ball State University. Stedman prided himself on being "interested and involved in many things."

In Stedman, Oprah found the kind of companion she needed. He was fun to go out with. He enjoyed playing tennis, golf, skiing, and most sports, and did them all well. "I don't like being average in anything," he said in an interview for *EM*.

Oprah Winfrey could look to the coming months with confidence. Her days were busier than ever. After a strenuous morning of hosting her show, she would stand to greet and shake hands with studio guests. She had learned how much this meant to them.

As her schedule became increasingly complex, she was forced to make adjustments. Oprah could no longer do many things personally that had once given her more direct contact with her fans. She still spoke often at community-related events. She remained meticulous in seeing that letters to her received an answer, but she now maintained a staff to help her handle the volume of mail.

After she completes planning for the next day's show, she is finally free to go home. Oprah has learned how to put the "R" in relax. She has told how she will turn on the gold spigot on her bathtub, the spigot shaped like a swan, fill the tub, and soak in the water made fragrant and bubbly with bath oil. She may get into comfortable floral pajamas and pull on heavy socks. After that, she may curl up in a chair, or on the bench under a window that overlooks Lake Shore Drive.

This is a far cry from life on a farm in Kosciusko. Sometimes, Oprah has said, she thinks about this. She thinks about it and says with thankfulness, "Good Lord, I do feel blessed."

12

Moving with the Flow of Life

Oprah Winfrey awakens early each morning. She gets out of bed even earlier than necessary to be on time for her show. This quiet time, she says, helps her to get ready for whatever the day will bring.

From the broad windows in her high-rise home she can watch the sunrise over Lake Michigan — that great link in America's waterway system, which stretches east to the Atlantic Ocean and south toward the Mississippi River. The view of the lake Indians called "Big Water" brings a moment of calm. The way Oprah sees it, this time of quiet meditation is invaluable.

Once Oprah leaves home, her life is conditioned by the busy schedule of an entertainment star who is also a business woman. Nineteen eighty-seven prolonged and expanded the acclaim and accomplishment of the year before. Despite the praise and money-making, the talk-show host tried to steer a steady course. As she said, she kept "moving with the flow of life."

If the flow of life brought challenges, she faced them head-on. For her television shows, Oprah Winfrey never backed away from controversial topics. If she felt strongly that her viewing audience would be interested, or should be better informed about the subject, she considered presenting it. An example of this gutsy outlook was her decision to take her show south and to explore feelings in an extraordinary racial conflict that made newspaper headlines. She decided to take *The Oprah Winfrey Show* to Forsyth County, in Georgia.

Is she out of her skull? some viewers asked. They became alarmed for Oprah's safety.

Wouldn't it be better to bring a group from Forsyth County to the studio in Chicago? This was another question viewers asked.

Oprah and her staff had thought over all such options and made a final decision. If the people of the United States could see and hear the segregationists in Forsyth County, then perhaps people would better understand the depth of their racial bigotry. Also, people could see whether everyone in Forsyth County had the same racist attitudes.

The stories from the Georgia county had unfolded in newspaper, magazine, and television coverage. They told of persisting deep-seated racist attitudes and practices of a kind that the civil rights movement, inspired by Dr. Martin Luther King, Jr. had tried to end forever.

Forsyth County did not have a single African American living within its borders. Many Forsyth citizens seemed determined to keep the racial pattern that way.

A group of civil rights activists decided to challenge them. As part of the official commemoration of the birthday of Dr. Martin Luther King, Jr., in January 1987, a protest march was planned to focus media attention on the racial problem in the all-white county. Leading the march was Reverend Hosea Williams, a veteran fighter for civil rights. Years before, he had led a successful movement to desegregate public facilities in Savannah, Georgia. Hosea Williams had crusaded with Dr. King in most major nonviolent movements all the way to Memphis. He appears with Dr. King in a famous photo

Oprah in one of her pensive moods.

taken on the same motel balcony where the leader was assassinated a day later.

Forsyth County held no fears for Reverend Williams when he led an interracial "Brotherhood March" to protest the county's exclusion of blacks. But nobody knew what would happen when black people set foot on Forsyth soil.

The news brought out members of the Ku Klux Klan and other segregationist groups. They came waving Confederate flags and flaunting signs that let the world know how they felt about the action:

GO HOME NIGGER!
WHITE CIVIL RIGHTS!

That was not all. Some of the segregationists became so angry they began to throw rocks and mud and bottles at the peaceful protesters.

The drama from Forsyth County continued. Coretta Scott King, who has continued the civil rights crusading begun by her martyred husband, helped to lead a massive "Anti-intimidation March" the next week to protest the violence. Some twenty thousand people participated.

Oprah Winfrey studied the conflict taking place in Georgia. The problem presented the type of issue that should be exposed in public debate. She decided to use her show as a forum.

At first the plan called for representatives from both sides to present their views on the same show. After considerable study, Oprah and her staff decided that the possibility of violence was too risky. Tempers might explode in the TV studio. Also, a direct confrontation could bring so much shouting and heated words that any reasonable dialogue would be impossible.

The final decision resulted in a plan that would focus upon feelings and information, and avoid confrontation. *The Oprah*

Winfrey Show decided to let residents of Forsyth County give the nation their reasons for excluding minority citizens.

Guidelines were specific. The only people to be considered for the studio audience would be those who could prove that they were residents of Forsyth County. That automatically excluded all African Americans.

Strong protest came from civil rights activists. Oprah would be airing only one side of the problem, they said.

Oprah gave her logical reason. "I view this as a unique opportunity to explore the thoughts and feelings of the community in light of recent events," she said. She explained that there were indeed people who were seen throwing rocks. But there were no doubt others, too, who were ashamed of those who threw the rocks. The American people should hear from both sides, she insisted.

So Oprah Winfrey took her show to a county where members of her race had not been allowed to live since 1912. The viewing interest became intense in all sections of the country. Some workers took the day off, wanting to see the telecast as it took place.

The show was telecast from a restaurant in Cumming, about forty miles north of Atlanta. Oprah took her television production crew, and all her staff there. The restaurant, called The Dinner Deck, became the studio.

It was Oprah alone, however, who stood among the sea of white faces and calmly set forth the purpose of the broadcast. "We are here simply to ask why Forsyth County has not allowed black people to live here in seventy-five years."

Forsyth citizens told how the ban began. In 1912, a white woman was allegedly raped by three black men. All three of the accused men were lynched. Word went out that all other blacks must get out of Forsyth County. Since that day no non-white persons had been welcomed.

Oprah permitted the diehard racists to have their say about "niggers" and "communists." She also allowed Forsyth citizens with a different view to be heard. Many citizens saw the practice as wrong. One person asked that Forsyth County not be judged by the bigotry of the extremists. A woman revealed that she had marched along with the civil rights demonstrators. The people in the studio audience who pleaded for racial harmony outnumbered the ones who advocated white supremacy.

For days after the telecast from Forsyth County, viewers were still talking about Oprah and how she had dared take her show into Klan territory. A newspaper columnist dubbed the talk-show host a "one-woman ambassador, surely the most curious Southern belle many whites inside the restaurant had ever seen."

Just as memorable as this show are many less publicized gems — the ones that Oprah's fans talk about over and over. The program that featured Bill Cosby as guest was one of these. Most times Oprah builds her show around topics or issues of interest. Every now and then, however, she highlights a big-name personality. When promotions announced the date for Cosby's appearance, the studio phones rang constantly with calls from people who wanted to reserve a seat and be a part of the studio audience.

The program proved a delight. The two people rated among the most popular and highest-paid entertainers on television simply talked together. Oprah did not quiz Cosby, nor probe as she does with some guests. She sat back and let him "do his thing." The range of topics was extraordinary. In his calm, philosophical style, Cosby talked about his children and about the quirks of family life. He heaped praises upon his wife, Camille, for her quiet strength. He told jokes about himself, and balanced these with painful episodes in his life. Oprah, like her audience, was mesmerized.

One point which piqued everyone's interest was the caution Bill Cosby gave regarding the handling of finances. He told how early on in his life he and his wife lost money when he entrusted many of the financial aspects of his affairs to others. His advice to Oprah, and to the audience, was given in four words: "Sign Your Own Checks!" This meant every check, he emphasized, from the laundry bill on up. Oprah promised to heed his advice.

Shows that deal with dieting are always sure to draw large listening-viewing audiences. Admirers knew of Oprah's continuing battle to lose weight. Other weight watchers were always anxious to offer their suggestions.

Oprah joked freely about her hefty size. The extra weight she had put on for the role of Sofia in *The Color Purple* stayed on. Her weight hovered around 190 pounds. She joked about the many diets she had tried, and evoked the days she had begun a diet with "just a boiled egg," only to succumb by morning's end to a calorie-laden lunch. Sympathizing fans shared their favorite diets in hopes of helping her slim down.

Why is Oprah so special to so many people? Studio guests and home viewers alike agree upon one secret of Oprah's phenomenal popularity. She makes people feel as though *their* problems are *her* problem. She is especially attuned to women and the pressures they face from so many sides. She tells these women, in effect: I understand; I care about you. Perhaps after we've talked, and listened, your life will change.

Young people, children and teenagers, are important to Oprah Winfrey. She predicates many shows upon the problems they face in today's world. When the public school teachers of Chicago were on strike in 1987, one of the guests on Oprah's show was a student. He expressed his concern over the fact that the strike was causing him to miss valuable classroom instruction. Other guests on this show were teachers, parents, and union officials. Oprah let the student know that his voice, his views, and his perspective as a student were as valid as those of any other guest. She made sure the youth received equal time and coverage.

On the shows that deal with current problems such as drugs, Oprah makes sure that young people also have a chance to speak their minds. On these telecasts, such as the program dealing with teen pregnancies, Oprah speaks with passion to young people in the studio, and those watching from other places. The young years should be enjoyed, she tells them. These years must be spent in learning. Oprah reminds young listeners that the older years, past their teens, will be time enough for such adult responsibilities as having babies.

Oprah's attention to young people extends beyond her television show. As part of her community service in Chicago, she and several friends took a special interest in a group of young girls who live in the Cabrini-Green housing project. Chicago's sixteen-stories-high Cabrini-Green has been beset by all the ills of many big-city housing projects for poor families, including murder, rape, and drug-dealing. This is the environment in which young boys and girls—beautiful, young, innocent, gifted—must try to survive.

Out of her own experience, Oprah knows the danger that this kind of environment can stifle creativity and initiative. She encourages the children of Cabrini-Green and children facing problems in similar living conditions to prevail over their surroundings.

As a project, Oprah chose several young people to receive special attention. She gave them glimpses of another style of living. They went to her apartment for slumber parties. They experienced the joy of fun-filled shopping trips. Oprah even took some of them to Tennessee for a visit. She made it clear to these little "sisters" that if they brought home D's or F's on their report card, they were out of the group.

In talking with groups of teenage girls, Oprah reminds them of what their lives might be like if they became mothers. A life with little education, no skills, and no goals would be a dead end.

"Don't tell me you want to lead exciting, productive lives and then say you can't say 'No' to some boy," Oprah preaches to teenage audiences. "If you want something to love and hug tell me! I'll buy you a puppy!"

During many weekends, Oprah has been seen speaking before church and community groups. She offers forceful advice to everyone, but especially for the young. Get an education! Set goals for yourself! Through Oprah's generosity several students have received scholarships to the Chicago Academy of Arts where their natural talents can be encouraged and refined.

Oprah makes it clear to these students that they must strive for excellence, not only in schoolwork, but also in other areas of their lives as well. She pushes them to realize their highest potential.

Remembering how books have influenced her own development, Oprah stresses the importance of reading when she speaks to young people. She reminds them how the years of reading since childhood contributed to her command of language, her ability to think and her composure with all types of people.

Oprah Winfrey was certainly a fitting choice as one of the celebrities picked by the American Library Association for a promotional program to encourage reading. In a series of colorful posters, each celebrity is pictured enjoying a good read.

The poster featuring Oprah shows her in lovely Grant Park, the center link in a chain of lakeshore parks that add to Chicago's unique charm. Framed by a background of clear blue skies and white sails dotting Lake Michigan, Oprah sits on the grass under a tree and reads the book she describes as her number-one all-time favorite: *Their Eyes Were Watching God.* This story is written by the masterful storyteller Zora Neale Hurston. The author presents black folk culture through poetic fiction. Her main character, Janie, typifies a woman who faces the quest for true identity and fulfillment.

With so many irons burning hot in the fire, Oprah managed to

Oprah Winfrey in the widely publicized American Library Association poster
urges young people to join in her favorite pastime — reading.

keep her TV talk show at a level that won top ratings. The smooth running of *The Oprah Winfrey Show* is due in part to the loyalty of staff members who are dedicated to Oprah and to her show's success. Most of the staff are young; the majority are women. All are efficient. If they prove otherwise, Oprah says, they are out!

Staff members came with Oprah to Baltimore, Maryland in November, 1988 to broadcast *The Oprah Winfrey Show* from Southwestern High School. Students, parents, and teachers packed the huge gymnasium, transformed into a production studio. The topic showed Oprah's continued interest in the problems faced by young people. She guided students in discussing voilence in public schools.

Trim and vivacious in a pretty blue dress, Oprah moved easily among the guests, actually seeming a part of the audience. "One of the reasons we are here is because I am personally concerned about the education of young people," she said. Students lined up for the rare chance to be seen and heard on Oprah's show.

During her Baltimore visit Oprah met privately with a group of student leaders. Her message to them was clear: ". . . we are responsible for our lives." She advised them to help stop school disruptions by saying, "Look, we are not going to tolerate this. Our education is important to us, and we are not going to have this go on in our schools." That, Oprah said, is when violence will end.

Oprah Winfrey continued to move in high gear, but with steady purpose. "I try to move with the flow of life," she said, "and not to dictate what life should be for me, but just let it flow."

The current of Oprah's life has affected the direction of countless other lives that she has touched through word or action. "My mission," she said, "is to use this position, power, and money to create opportunities for other people."

13

Dreams and Missions

"I'm going to fly! I know it!"

As Oprah made this prediction for her future, her hazel eyes sparkled and she laughed with the joy of a woman on the move with things going her way.

Marcia Ann Gilespie of *Ms.* magazine recalled how Oprah made this prediction in an interview. The two talked together in Oprah's office at the Chicago-based company she owns — Harpo Productions, Inc. The letters in HARPO, seen in reverse order, spell OPRAH. She first set Harpo up in 1986. The company has expanded since then, and now launches and manages all Oprah's business ventures.

One of Oprah's goals in establishing her own production company is to bring to the screen some of the most powerful books written by and about African Americans. In preparation for this she has already bought the screen rights to several bestselling books. Many of these works are about African-American women.

Toni Morrison's novel, *Beloved*, published in 1987, was a Book-of-the-Month-Club main selection; it also won the Pulitzer

Prize. Oprah's production company has purchased the rights to bring this blockbuster of a book to the public via the screen.

The setting for *Beloved* is Ohio during the period after the Civil War. Sethe, the central character, is an escaped slave, a woman of "iron eyes and backbone to match." The novel follows Sethe's struggle to overcome the dark tragedies of her earlier life, her fight in "beating back the past," in order to shape a future. Oprah admits that she would love to play the part of Sethe — a role, she says, that she "was born to play."

Oprah's production company has also bought the movie rights to other books. When Oprah read the international bestselling autobiography, *Kaffir Boy*, she immediately got in touch with the author, Mark Mathabane. She had him as a guest on her talk show. She did more. She brought members of his family from South Africa to the United States for a visit and a taste of freedom. The reunion of the author and his grandmother, mother, sisters and a brother was filmed at the airport and publicized. Young readers rushed to libraries for copies of *Kaffir Boy*.

The story pictures the author's boyhood in the ghettos of South Africa where, because of the apartheid system, his family continually faced starvation. Apartheid is a system of racial segregation that discriminates politically and economically against all non-whites. Mathabane tells how he used to rummage through garbage thrown out by white families and go to the slaughterhouses to get blood from the animals killed so they could boil it for soup and stay alive.

In America, Mathabane was helped by scholarships to get an education in New York colleges. He dreamed of bringing his family to stay permanently in America so they could enjoy the freedom he found. In his writings, the young South African author, who now teaches in a college, stresses over and over his belief in the strongest weapon against oppression: EDUCATION!

Oprah had also bought production rights to a novel that had won rave reviews when it was published in 1983. The author, Gloria Naylor, was studying on a fellowship at Yale University when she wrote most of the book. The plot uses the device of intertwining the stories of seven African-American women from varied backgrounds. They live in a tenement on a dead-end unpaved street in a northern ghetto — the street called Brewster Place. Each woman, in a different way, struggles against poverty while bright dreams fade. In the end, each of the women has to learn how to take control of her life and work to abolish all the Brewster Places of the big cities.

Oprah Winfrey decided to bring Gloria Naylor's challenging story of conflict, love, and survival to a wide audience through the medium of television. She convinced ABC that the novel would appeal to viewers. After that, Harpo and Oprah worked out a deal for coproducing the series.

Oprah also played the lead role of Mattie Michael, whose life begins the novel. Oprah tells how, reading the book on the set of *The Color Purple*, she decided that the story was one she would like to have a part in portraying.

As it turned out, Oprah became both a star and co-executive producer of the TV movie. Together with the producer, she put together a cast dedicated to making the film a hit. It included Cicely Tyson, Olivia Cole, Robin Givens, Yvonne Stickney, Lonette McKie, Paula Kelly, Lynn Whitfield, Jackee — and Oprah.

The miniseries *The Women of Brewster Place* was aired March 1989. Many television viewers who were not familiar with Oprah's lifelong interest in acting were surprised at her masterful performance. "She shines in an all-star cast," wrote Michael Hill in the *Baltimore Sun* evening edition. Oprah plays Mattie, who starts as a twenty-year-old girl, passes through successive stages of her life, and ends as a fifty year old woman, beaten down by circumstances but ready to take charge of her life anew, and in the process help other women.

When Oprah dons a gray wig, puts on an apron, and begins speaking in her expressive voice, she "becomes" Mattie Michael.

Through the years, Oprah's mother has followed her daughter's phenomenal success with pride. Mother and daughter have grown to understand each other better and have learned how to have fun together. Oprah has bought Vernita Lee a lovely condominium in Milwaukee where she could have the kind of life enjoyed by the families she once worked for as a maid. When Vernita visits Oprah in Chicago, the two may sit and chat, or enjoy a game of backgammon, or munch on one of Oprah's favorite snacks — microwave popcorn.

In Nashville, Tennessee, Vernon Winfrey is understandably proud of his only child. In his barbershop he keeps a television set so that he can watch his daughter's show along with his customers. They share his pride.

Vernon Winfrey has taken it all in his steady stride. Once when Oprah reminded him that she was wealthy and could give him any gift he wanted, he laughed and told her he only needed new tires for his truck. Another time, when he wanted a ticket to the Michael Spinks–Mike Tyson heavyweight title fight, Oprah saw that he got one.

Longtime friends who are customers sometimes tease Vernon Winfrey as they watch his daughter's show on his large television screen. "Who's that girl?" a customer may ask.

"She does look kind of familiar to me," the barber will reply with a chuckle. Sometimes Velma Winfrey, who helped him guide their daughter through the teen years, watches *The Oprah Winfrey Show* with her husband and joins in the fun.

In addition to the barbershop, Vernon Winfrey owns other properties and is involved in several other business ventures. In 1975, Oprah's father was elected a member of the Metro Council, representing Nashville's Fifth District. He is still a staunch church worker and a deacon in Faith-United Missionary Baptist Church.

114

Whenever Oprah telephones her father to say she will come home, the visit becomes a joyful time for father and daughter. During one visit they decided to go back to Oprah's roots, back to Kosciusko, to relive old times. "I celebrate my upbringing," Oprah says. She is thankful that she was raised by her grandmother the first six years, then sent to live with her mother and then with her father. Because of her life in these diverse environments, she believes she is better able to understand problems other people are facing. She brings this empathy to her talk show.

A proud moment for father and daughter was the day Oprah Winfrey completed the project that met her last course requirement. She was officially awarded her college degree by Tennessee State University.

Oprah proved her belief in the value of education by establishing four-year scholarships for ten students to attend her alma mater. Her daddy looked on with pride as she announced that the scholarships would be named, in his honor, as the Vernon Winfrey Scholarships. "No person," she said, "has had a greater influence in extolling the importance and value of a good education than my father. It is because of him that I am where I am today." Oprah Winfrey had been chosen to deliver the commencement address to the 625 graduating seniors.

In giving the scholarships, Oprah set guidelines for the students who received them. She selected the ten recipients from the incoming first-year students. Her choices were based upon need for the money, and scholastic ability. These scholarships cover everything — tuition, books, room and board, even spending money. Each student has to keep up at least a B average. These students understand that if their grades fall below par, they are liable to be warned by their donor. Oprah thinks of these students as an extended part of her own family, she says.

Her father's keen sense of business seems to have been passed along to his daughter. Recently, Oprah shocked the business and entertainment world by announcing another of her "whammo" deals. Harpo, Inc., had bought *The Oprah Winfrey Show.* Oprah would take over the ownership and production of the show from WLS-TV, the ABC Station that brought Oprah to Chicago. King World would continue to syndicate it, and for at least five years it would remain at ABC.

How much would Oprah make in a season? People were curious. According to the "Smart Money" section of *Ms.* magazine "Many estimate her take will be over 40 million dollars."

Oprah speaks philosophically about her multimillionaire status, according to Marcia Gillespie in *Ms.* "The deal itself doesn't mean anything. Unless you choose to do great things with it, it makes no difference how much you are rewarded or who much power you have. I want to live up to what this represents."

Oprah continues to fly. She has bought her own studio in Chicago. Her plan for the 88,000 square foot space, she told *Ms.*, is to create a stimulating and comfortable environment that will include an exercise room and a complete kitchen, with dining area and a full-time cook. Oprah wants people to love to come to work. Her combined television and production ventures are now known as Harpo Studios, Inc.

The brilliant attorney who has been advising Oprah on her financial projects is Jeffrey Jacobs. He met Oprah soon after she came to Chicago and began searching for a local entertainment lawyer. Jacobs became a chief adviser. Fortunately, he seems to agree with the advice once given to Oprah by Bill Cosby — "Sign Your Own Checks." According to *Ms.* magazine, attorney Jacobs says, "She signs the checks, she makes the decisions."

Plans and projects for Oprah seem to be always expanding, always evolving. She has announced plans for a minority program which would bring more people into the television and film industry as producers. Another plan would establish a retreat for women, a place Oprah sees as "an extension of what we do for an hour on the show. I want to be able to spread the message that you are responsible for your own life and to set up a format to teach people how to do that."

Despite her phenomenal successes, Oprah recently recognized that she faced a challenge in her own life. Her body was still carrying around too much fat! Oprah tipped the scales around 190 pounds. This was too much weight.

Oprah had often joked about her weight gain during her shows. She joked that she went from size tens to size twelves — and all the way to elastics. She kept her size-ten jeans hanging in her closet. One day, she promised herself, she would wear size ten again.

She later recalled the evening she made a firm decision. Oprah was enjoying dinner with some close friends. She was having her usual good time with food. Suddenly she noticed that her friend's husband was not eating, and asked him why. He explained that he was on a twelve-week diet that allowed him only a high protein drink five times a day. Along with the protein, he explained, dieters were taught to use behavior modification.

Oprah became intrigued, she told her audience, recalling the times she had lost pounds only to gain them back. She joined a special diet designed for people who should lose at least fifty pounds. The program dealt with more than mere weight loss. It also tackled physical, social, and emotional problems that may arise from being severely overweight.

Oprah joined the program and used the kind of self-control she talks about on her shows. At the end of eighteen weeks, she lost sixty-seven pounds!

One day, on *The Oprah Winfrey Show*, the host suddenly threw off her jacket. There, for all her viewers to see, was a gorgeous, svelte Oprah in a, yes, size-ten of Calvin Klein jeans. She explained that size ten in Calvin Klein may be equivalent to size eight in many other brands.

Oprah celebrated her triumph with her studio audience. She had been a food addict, she confessed. "This whole weight-loss attempt was my effort to gain self-control," she said.

It is important to remember that the type of liquid diet used by Oprah should be tried only under strict supervision. It must never be undertaken without a personal screening and complete physical examination. Patients who qualify are observed closely and must pay periodic visits to the clinic to ensure that the weight loss is medically safe.

For Oprah, the successful weight loss represented a great triumph. As she told an interviewer for *Women's Day* magazine, "I feel like a caterpillar that has broken its shell."

Daily exercise is necessary to keep from regaining the weight. This was no problem for Oprah. She told Nanay Griffin of *US* magazine, "I have to get up at five in order to run six miles." When asked if this was tough for her, Oprah replied, "No. It's the price I pay to keep the weight off. It was the deal I made with myself." She talks wrily of all the things she once bought to encourage exercise — goggles, lovely swim suits, swimming caps, cute tennis outfits. She would use them a few times and then the novelty would wear off. "So," she says, "running is the most consistent thing I do."

Just as millions of people admire Oprah, there are some people for whom she voices tremendous admiration. One of these is the Reverend Jesse Jackson.

Judy Markey of *Woman's Day* recently sat with Oprah in the high-rise office at Harpo Production Company and "pinned her down" on issues of our times. The two kicked off their shoes and began talking.

At one point Oprah happened to mention Jesse Jackson. Judy Markey followed with a question. "Suppose he called you up and said, Oprah, I'm taking a look at the next eight years for black people and trying to figure out where I fit in. What do you think I should do?"

Oprah threw back her head and laughed. "Jesse Jackson calls

Oprah reveals to the nation the results of her diet success, wearing size ten jeans.

ME? Boy, is that a hoot." She grew serious. She and Jackson know each other well. "Jesse Jackson has done a great thing for this country because he represents hope to people who would otherwise be hopeless," Oprah said. "I don't mean just black people and I don't mean just poor people."

That same year, the *Ebony* annual reader's poll voted Oprah the Most Admired Black Woman. The poll also voted Jesse Jackson the Most Admired Black Man.

Oprah's popularity with a nationwide audience, along with her varied achievements, have won her recognition from many quarters.

Some of this recognition has come in words of praise. In a general review of her show in *TV Guide*, Don Merrell suggested to readers, "If you haven't yet treated yourself to *The Oprah Winfrey Show*, we suggest that you do so soon. The woman's warmth alone makes her a natural for television." Merrill reminded readers that "beneath a homey personality that invites confidence, there is a confident, talented journalist digging for truth."

Oprah has also won the coveted Daytime Emmy Award as best talk-show host, and *The Oprah Winfrey Show* won the Emmy for best talk show.

Friends and critics alike try to guess the next phase in Oprah Winfrey's life, on a business as well as a social level. In whichever direction she turns, they wager, she will be a trailblazer, and she will be doing something to inspire and help others.

One of Oprah's recent business ventures is a classy Chicago restaurant, "The Eccentric." A visitor who went to check out the place at 159 West Erie, just west of Chicago's "Magnificent Mile," was impressed with the sophisticated atmosphere. The Eccentric has become a popular spot for after-work crowds.

The diners are a blend of professional and cultural groups. They enter through a marbled foyer decorated with paintings and sketches depicting life in the great cities of the world — Paris, London, Chicago, Rome.

In the cocktail lounge, waiters and waitresses stroll around with complimentary hors d'oeuvres for diners waiting for the first dinner seating. Women are very much in evidence among the staff — a part of Oprah's determination to keep women in the forefront of the work force.

Once seated in the dining area, with its upholstered chairs, dinner guests choose from a wide range of appetizers, sumptuous salads, sandwiches, vegetables, entrees, and desserts. The printed

Oprah Winfrey and Jesse Jackson, sharing a moment of friendship.

menu adds a polite reminder for those who care to smoke: Please adjourn to the bar.

Oprah also bought a new home. An article by Brain Haugh in an issue of the *Star* was illustrated by a picture of the chateau-style country home located in Rolling Prairie, Indiana, approximately two hours by car from Chicago. The house has a helicoptor paid, riding stables, tennis courts, and a swimming pool. Oprah has reportedly been seen jogging down the road in a bright-red track suit, according to the occupants of a neighboring house. Oprah's mom, Vernita Lee, has reportedly moved into a cottage on the grounds.

The lavish rooms inside include a nursery and a toddler's playroom. Oprah frankly acknowledges her dream of one day having a baby of her own.

The sprawling, 160-acre country home in Indiana, may remind her in many ways of the early years she spent on her grandmother's Mississippi farm. Through the years, Oprah has said her dream house would be on a farm. "I'll have horses," she would say, "golden retrievers, and two children, maybe. One, for sure . . . and a garden . . . ."

Years later Oprah returned to her roots, and went back to Mississippi. The road that runs in front of the house in which she was born was renamed. Oprah was invited to come for the ceremonies. On a lovely spring day, as three hundred onlookers cheered and clapped, Oprah cut the ribbon and the road was officially rededicated as "Oprah Winfrey Road."

Oprah Winfrey has caught the fancy of the world. Within a few years she has become more than a household word. She is more like a folk hero.

Life and dreams flow so spectacularly well for Oprah that some admirers worry about this. What if the bubble bursts? What if her show loses popularity?

Oprah Winfrey gives reassuring answers about her future. She faces the coming years with a rock-firm belief and says, "There are grander days to come." She is confident, she says, because she has stable roots.

She sees her work now as a form of ministry, inspiring people, encouraging the despondent, and giving them a feeling of hope. If she can help people to feel a little better about their day, or about the way they treat others, then she has helped them.

During all the years since her Baltimore days, Oprah has had a confidante in a close friend, Gail King Bumpus. The two young newscasters became friends one night when a heavy snowstorm hit Baltimore and Oprah invited Gail to spend the night at her apartment, not far from the television station. The two have been close friends ever since. Oprah is godmother to both of Gail's young children.

Recently, Oprah appeared in a prime-time television special, *Just Between Friends*. Oprah invited Gail King Bumpus, her friend of thirteen years, to be her special guest and illustrate true friendship.

By the closing of the 1980s Oprah Winfrey had deepened her mission of public service, especially in the area of educating young people. She became a popular choice by college students to be their commencement speaker. Oprah also donated one million dollars to establish the Oprah Winfrey Endowment Scholarship Fund at Morehouse College in Atlanta, Georgia, the school from which Dr. Martin Luther King, Jr. and his sons graduated. Morehouse honored Oprah's accomplishments by awarding her an honorary doctorate. She received a Doctor of Humane Letters degree at the commencement exercises.

Oprah Gail Winfrey faces the 1990s still moving with the flow of life. News articles and illustrations show the changing focus of her plans. They no longer deal primarily with such topics as glamour, publicitiy, clothes, etc. Oprah is often featured for her business ventures, or for her humanitarian pursuits—educating students, helping women to reach their potential, and inspiring the hopless to take hold of their lives.

Her lifestyle remains classy. According to the March 6, 1990 issue of *Star*, Oprah has purchased an entire floor of a Chicago lakeside condominium to convert it into a penthouse mansion, with eight bedrooms and ten bathrooms.

And she is still winning awards. In January, 1990, NBC-TV televised the ceremonies for the prestigious Image Awards, presented annually by the National Association for the Advancement of Colored People (NAACP). The Beverly Hills/Hollywood Branch of the NAACP gives the awards annually to honor those who have contributed to the positive portrayal of the black experience, and to expand opportunities in the entertainment field. Oprah won *four* Image Awards: Entertainer of the Year, co-producer of *The Women of Brewster Place*, an award for her role in the same production, and one for the *No Man Dies Alone* segment of *Prime Time Oprah*. Vernon Winfrey was present to hug his daughter and share her tears of joy.

Oprah continues to fly, and to provide inspiration for countless other persons young and old. Many people have asked this remarkable woman to describe herself. One of her answers is intriguing: "I am just a woman striving. Striving to magnify the Lord. That's all." To another person she described herself in three words: "I'm just me."

Chronology

1954 — Oprah Gail Winfrey is born in Kosciusko, Mississippi, on January 29.

1968 — Oprah moves from her mother's home in Milwaukee, Wisconsin, to her father's home in Nashville, Tennessee.

1970 — As president of the student council, Oprah attends the White House Council on Youth.

1971 — Oprah becomes the first black girl to win Nashville's Miss Fire Prevention contest.

Radio station WVOL in Nashville hires Oprah as a part-time newscaster.

Oprah graduates from East High School and enters Tennessee State University on a scholarship given by the Elks.

1972 — After being named Miss Black Nashville and Miss Black Tennessee, Oprah goes to California to compete for Miss Black America.

Station WTVF-TV in Nashville hires Oprah to co-anchor the evening and weekend news while she continues her studies.

1976 — WJZ-TV, Baltimore, hires Oprah to co-host the local evening news.

1978 — WJZ-TV teams Oprah with Richard Sher as co-host of its new morning talk show, *People Are Talking*.

1984 — WLS-TV in Chicago chooses Oprah to host a failing talk show called *A.M. Chicago*.

1985 — Oprah is given the role of Sofia in the movie *The Color Purple*.

A.M. Chicago is expanded from thirty to sixty minutes and renamed *The Oprah Winfrey Show*.

1986 — Baltimore honors Oprah with the city's first "Celebrity Award."

Oprah is nominated to receive an Academy Award for her supporting role in *The Color Purple*.

Oprah plays a leading role in the movie *Native Son*.

Stedman Graham becomes a steady dating partner for Oprah.

The Oprah Winfrey Show is syndicated nationally.

In *Ebony* magazine's annual readers' poll, Oprah is voted the most admired black woman.

1987 — The American Library Association selects Oprah, a "celebrity reader," to help promote reading.

Oprah establishers "The Vernon Winfrey Scholarships" to help educate students at Tennessee State University.

Oprah sweeps the Daytime Emmy Awards, winning in the categories of best talk show host and best talk show.

1988 — Oprah expands Harpo, Inc. into a production company and buys the screen rights to several bestselling books, many by African-American authors.

The radio and television industry names Oprah Winfrey the Broadcaster of the Year.

Oprah serves as co-executive producer and stars in a lead role in the miniseries *The Women of Brewster Place*.

1989 — Oprah establishes a one million dollar scholarship fund at Morehouse College in Atlanta, Georgia.

Oprah purchases a 160-acre farm in Rolling Prairie, Indiana.

Oprah appears with best friend Gail King Bumpus in a syndicated prime-time special, *Just Between Friends*.

1990 — The National Association for the Advancement of Colored People (NAACP) honors Oprah with four Image Awards.

Index

A *All My Children*, 64, 65
  A.M. Chicago, 20, 21, 66, 69, 70
  ABC (American Broadcasting
    Company), 58
  American Library Association,
    108, *109*
  Angelou, Maya, 23, 35, *39*
  apartheid, 112
  Applefield, Floraine, 83
  A Tale of Two Cities, 25

B Baltimore, Maryland, 57, 58, 60,
    61
  Baltimore Sun, 59, 75, 113
  Beloved, 111, 112
  Brown vs. Board of Education, 7
  Browning, Elizabeth Barrett, 86
  Bumpus, Gail King, 123
  Burch, Dr. Janet, 48

C Cabrini-Green housing project,
    107
  Chapman, Harry, 53
  Chicago, 66, 68-71
  Clark, Chris, 51, 52
  Color Purple, The, 75-79, 81-85,
    89, 106, 126
  CBS (Columbia Broadcasting
    System), 51
  Cosby, Bill, 90, 105
  Costa Rica, 18, 19
  Cox, Dr. William, 52, 53
  Crystal, Billy, *72*
  custody, 19

D Daytime Emmy Award, 120
  Dexter Avenue Baptist Church, 9
  Dickens, Charles, 25
  DiMaio, Debra (Debbie), 66

E East High School, 34, 35, 46
  Easter speech, 11
  Ebony magazine, 68, 94, 120
  Eccentric, The, 120-121
  EM magazine, 98
  Essence magazine, 21

F Faith-United Missionary Baptist
    Church, 114
  Forsyth County, Georgia, 101,
    103-105
  Franklin, Aretha, 29
  Freedom Delegates, 80
  Freedom Movement, 21
  Freedom Ride, 21

G Goldberg, Whoopi, 78, 83
  Graham, Stedman, 95, *96*, 97, 98
  Grauman's Chinese Theater, 42

H Hamer, Fannie Lou, 79, 80, 81
  Harpo Productions, Inc., 111,
    116, 126
  Heidelberg, John, 42, 43, 51, 52
  Hollywood, California, 42
  Hughes, Langston, 23
  Hurston, Zora Neale, 108

I *I Love Lucy*, 20

J Jackson, Jesse, 71, 118, 120, *121*
  Jacobs, Jeffrey, 116
  Jones, James Earl, *49*
  Jones, Quincy, 78, 79

K *Kaffir Boy*, 112
  Kennedy, John Fitzgerald, 22
  Kennedy, Robert Francis, 23
  King, Coretta Scott, 103
  King, Dr. Martin Luther, Jr., 9,
    21, 23, 70-71, 80,
    101
  King World Productions, Inc.,
    87, *88*
  Klein, Calvin, 117
  Kosciusko, Mississippi, 7, 9
  Kosciuko, 6, 7, *8*

L Lake Michigan, 100
  Larroquette, John, *72*
  Leave It To Beaver, 20
  Lee, Vernita, 9, 14, 15-17, 19,
    27, 31, 114, 122
  Lincoln High School, 24, *26*

M March of Dimes Campaign, 42
Markey, Judy, 118
Mathabane, Mark, 112
Metro Council, 114
Milwaukee, Wisconsin, 15, 16, 19, 24
Miss Black America, 48
Miss Black Nashville, 48
Miss Black Tennessee, 48
Miss Fire Prevention, 44, 45
Moore, Dudley, 72
Morehouse College, 123, 126
Morrison, Toni, 111
Ms. magazine, 111, 116

N Nashville, 16, 18, *30*, 32
Nashville Banner, The , 57
National Association for the Advancement of Colored People, 9, 124
Native Son, 84, 85
Naylor, Gloria, 113
Nicolet High School, 24

O "Operation Breadbasket," 71
"Oprah Winfrey Road," 122
Oprah Winfrey Show, The 87, 88, 89, 126
Orpah, 9
Otey, Anthony, 46
Outstanding Teenagers of America, 41

P *Parade* magazine, 31
People Are Talking, 64, 65, 66
Phil Donahue Show, The, 64, 65
Plessy vs. Ferguson, 7
Poag, Dr. Thomas, E., 47
Pugh, Willard, 78, 79
Pulitzer, Joseph, 76
Pulitzer Prize, 76

R Ross, Diana, 20, 23
reporting (television), *53*, 54, 55

S Schaefer, William Donald, 83
Scher, Richard, 64, 65, 83
segregation, 7, 71, 101, 103
sexual abuse, 20, 21, 77
Shriver, Maria, 85
Spielberg, Steven, 78, 79
Star magazine, 122
Supremes, The, 20, *22*
Swanson, Dennis, 66, 68, 69

T Tennessee State University, 47, *56*, 115
Their Eyes Were Watching God, 108
Truth, Sojourner, 36, *37*, *38*, 40, 79
Tubman, Harriet, 79, 80
Turner, Jerry, 59,*60*
Turner, Tina, 23
TV Guide, 120

U *US* magazine, 118

V *Variety* magazine, 92
Vernon Winfrey Scholarships, 115

W Walker, Alice, 75, 76, *77*
Walters, Barbara, 52
White House Conference on Youth, 41
Williams, Hosea, 101
Williams, Dr. Jamie, 47
Williams, Robin, 72
Winfrey, Hattie Mae, 10-13
Winfrey, Oprah
  acting career, 78, 83, 84, 85, 113
  broadcasting career, 43, 44, 47, 51-55, 57, 59, *60*, 61, 62, 87-89, 64-66, 116
  business ventures, 92, 111, 116, 120, 121
  childhood, 7, 10-13, 16-17
  education, 17, 24, 34, 35, 47, *56*, 115
  weight struggle, 73, 106, 117, *118*, *119*
Winfrey, Velma, 17, 19, 114
Winfrey, Vernon, 9, 16, 17, *18*, 19, 31, 32-34, 114, 115
Wisconsin, 15
WJZ-TV, 57, 58, 59, *60*, 64, 71, 72
WLS-TV, 66, 68, 69
Women's Day magazine, 118
Women of Brewster Place, The, 113, 126
Wright, Richard, 84
WTVF-TV, 51, 52, 57
WVOL, 42-44, 47, 49, 51